"At the heart of growing boundaries is growing a sense of self. Virginia Sobel brought herself from a grief-choked, thought-cloistered early life to full-flowering spiritual consciousness, and so can you—with the help of this lovely and powerful book. I heartily recommend it."

Anne Katherine
author of *Boundaries* and *Where to Draw the Line*

"Virginia Sobel's book shares her journey inward, as she moves away from being 'the woman with the cheesecake recipe,' to one who has a sense of her inner life and the meaning behind events unfolding in her life. Readers will enjoy her insights and learn how to view their lives with greater love and compassion. Enjoy this meaningful book!"

Meredith Young-Sowers, D.Div
author of *Wisdom Bowls* and the *Angelic Messenger Cards*

"Sobel's advice on working with Spirit and the Angelic Realm to heal the heart and mind is simply superb. This book is a must-read for anyone who is working to release the past and move forward in life with confidence, in the company of the Divine."

Denise Iwaniw
author of *Meditations from The Temple Within*

"Virginia Sobel has quite a story to tell. The courageous revelations of her heart urge us onward to begin our own journey of healing and wholeness. With a nurturing and supportive voice throughout, Sobel reassures us, 'If I can do it, you can do it too.' More than a personal tale of growth, this gentle but powerful book offers us truths to live by, as well as healing practices that can deepen our connection to self and Spirit."

Jan Deremo Lundy
author of *Coming Home to Ourselves* and *Awakening the Spirit Within*

"This valuable book gives us many useful tools to achieve self-acceptance and a higher spiritual awareness. I am honored to recommend this truly inspiring book."

Rev. J. Vaughn Boone
author of *Angels at Work*

"This book is a revealing look at life and the transformation possible through examining and learning from life's experiences. Virginia Sobel bravely shares herself in a most intimate way and reminds the reader that no matter how challenging the circumstance, there's always an opportunity for growth and awakening."

Laura V. Hyde
author of *Gifts of the Soul* and *The Intimate Soul*

"Sobel's writing is disarmingly honest. It is inspiring and practical, teaching us how to consciously partner with the Universe to create positive change in our lives."

Kay Nuyens, MA, C.Ht
author of *Invitation to Greatness—A workbook for personal growth*

"Sobel has written of her spiritual quest in such a manner that she grasps your attention on the first page and holds it throughout—a great read doesn't get any better than that! As Sobel shares her innermost feelings and experiences with us, we know that we are all one and the same, connected in both our sorrow and our joy. Know that this book came to you for a reason, and that sharing in Sobel's healing process will take you on a life-changing journey down a path full of tears, joy, awakenings, serenity, peace, and wholeness."

Karen Christopherson, MSW, CSW
author of *Karen's Intuitive Wisdom on Real-Life Questions:*
A Life Coach's Perspective

what good are you without your cheesecake recipe?

a spiritual journey toward self-worth

v i r g i n i a s o b e l

Spirit
Whispers
PRESS

Published by Spirit Whispers Press, P.O. Box 524, Grand Haven, Michigan 49417

Visit www.virginiasobel.com

Publishers Cataloging In Publication:

Sobel, Virginia, 1949–
    What good are you without your cheesecake recipe? : a spiritual journey toward self-worth / Virginia Sobel.
    p.   cm.
    Includes bibliographical references.
    ISBN 0-9740727-2-9 (pbk.)
    1.Spiritual healing. 2.Self-esteem. 3.Self-actualization (Psychology).
    I.Title.
    BV4598.2.S62 2003
    158.1—dc21   2003095920

dedication

I dedicate this book to Tom, my friend and husband, for holding my hand for 32 years,

and to Mandy and Matt, my children, for teaching me that I am capable of loving more deeply than I ever thought possible.

table of contents

acknowledgments

This book is a constant reminder to me of how generously my life has been blessed. I am deeply grateful to each of the following for the gifts they have given me:

To the Holy Spirit and my angels, for their guidance, inspiration, and ever-present love.

To Nelda Siegel and Norman Siegel, my mother and brother, who continue to support, love, and guide me from the other side.

To Martin Siegel, my father, for helping me learn such significant soul lessons.

To Phillip Siegel, Shirley Hoffmeyer, Frank Siegel, and Marlene Tompkins, my brothers and sisters (and dear friends). You are the very best gifts Mom and Dad could have ever given me. I love you all deeply.

To Laura Hyde, for believing in me and helping me learn how to believe in myself. Thank you for being a role model in living a life filled with compassion and integrity!

To Mary Trumpfheller, for being such a kind and loving mentor and treasured friend. You have helped me to birth not only this book, but also the real Virginia.

To Cindy Szymas and Kate McPolin, for your constant support, encouragement, and friendship. This book wouldn't have become a reality had it not been for you! My heart overflows with gratitude for the many contributions you have made to the editing, designing, and publishing of this book.

To Randy Borns of Borns LLC, for the creative genius that led to my face being on the cover of this book. "Trust me," you said and I did.

To David Wolters of David Alan Wolters Photography, for your photographic magic (and the lighting that makes me look 25!).

To Tom, for so generously spending hours proofreading drafts of the manuscript. Your precision and suggestions have made this book far better. Thank you, Hon!

To Mandy and Matt, for so graciously allowing me to share your personal experiences within the covers of this book. You are my greatest teachers.

To MaryAnn Graham and Mary Ann Rutherford, for reading book drafts and contributing valuable insights and feedback.

To Marcia Siegel, for seeing in me what I oftentimes couldn't see in myself.

To Susan and Nolan Clark, for being such incredible cheerleaders for my growth.

To Carol DeBlaey, for your constant encouragement during the long course of this project.

To Tena Crow, Nina Young, and Lynn Carter, for providing a safe emotional space for me to explore my feelings and beliefs. You have blessed my life!

To Aunt Norma (Rau) and Aunt Rachel (Veeneman), for spending hours with me fondly reminiscing about my mother and Norm.

To Mary Anne Zang and Kathy Forbes, for showing me how to take life a bit less seriously. Thank you for the gift of laughter.

To Judy Tindall, for contributing order and friendship to my life.

To my former Master Mind partners Mary Trumpfheller, Kay Nuyens, and Marguerite Weippert, for the guidance and encouragement that began this writing process.

To all of my friends and loved ones—past and present—who have so profoundly blessed my life. Each of you has left a unique imprint upon my heart. Your presence has made my life infinitely richer.

And last, but certainly not least, to all of the authors and teachers who have bravely revealed their own struggles so that others might benefit. Your courage has inspired me and changed my life.

I love you all.

prologue

I was driving recently when the LeeAnn Womack song "I Hope You'll Dance" came on the radio. I love this song because I find it so empowering. As I listened to the lyrics about a life filled with courage and passion, I began reflecting on earlier years. For much of my life, I wouldn't have been able to relate to Womack's words. The idea of "dancing" with life—of feeling light and enthusiastic and adventuresome—was something that held no meaning for me. I was far too busy just trying to cope.

By the time I was 22 my brother had committed suicide and my mother had died of cancer. These events were further compounded by a lifelong difficult relationship with my father. When I was 23, I began entertaining thoughts of suicide. "Dancing" with life was clearly out of the question.

Shame caused our family to lie about the circumstances of my brother's death. He was a Roman Catholic priest and suicide was unthinkable. Our secrecy prevented us from receiving the support of family and friends that we so desperately needed, and made it far more difficult for our family to heal.

In my 20s and early 30s I found it impossible to approach life with any degree of enthusiasm. I was struggling with the aftereffects of having lost two of the most important people in my life. I felt weighted down by unresolved grief, anger, and shame. Low self-esteem was my constant companion. To make matters worse, the emotional heaviness I felt led to my becoming physically overweight.

In an act of self-preservation, I began a journey that was to change my life. I set about questioning the way I perceived both the world and myself. I examined my spiritual beliefs, my attitudes, and my relationships. I began to understand the impact my spiritual beliefs had on my perceptions and my ability to heal. Bit by bit, step by step, I began to release the terrible emotional weight that I had carried around for so long.

What I learned, to quote inner-child expert John Bradshaw, was that "the only way out is through." I discovered we each have the ability to change our lives in ways that are nothing short of amazing. The key lies in acknowledging our personal pain and taking the steps—one by one—that will enable us to release it.

The book you are now holding started out as one of those steps. When I was in my 40s I received spiritual guidance to write about my life. The writing was suggested as a means of gaining more clarity about the experiences I had been through, the lessons I had learned from them, and the areas of my life that still held unresolved pain. The process was cathartic and gave me a new appreciation for how significantly I had changed.

I began to share with others what I had learned, and observed that the insights I was gaining were equally beneficial to them. It was then that I began transforming my personal writings into *What Good Are You Without Your Cheesecake Recipe? A Spiritual Journey Toward Self-Worth.*

I have written this book to share the lessons I have learned on my own journey to healing. I have also included, in Part 3, the activities that enabled me to integrate the lessons into my life. These steps have been nothing short of transformational for me. They have helped me discover an enthusiasm for life that I never before possessed. They have brought me much closer to being the person I always wanted to be.

I do not want to give you the mistaken impression, however, that I have "arrived" or even that such a thing is possible, for I don't believe it is. Life is a divine adventure with great purpose. There are always new insights to be had; new lessons to be learned about how to love ourselves and others more deeply.

I am tremendously grateful for the progress I have made thus far. The steps I have taken have helped me to feel lighter, freer, and more compassionate toward both others and myself. They have helped me to release many of the heavy emotional burdens I carried for so long.

It is my deepest hope that this book will assist you in taking your steps to emotional healing. It *can* be done. I am living proof of that! We *can* begin to understand the bigger picture and find great meaning and purpose in our lives. We *can* begin to recognize our divinity as empowered spiritual beings. We *can*, in the spirit of Womack's song, learn how to "Dance!"

Virginia Sobel

part 1

the beginning of my journey

chapter 1

looking for an answer

When my daughter was 4 years old, I worked at the preschool she attended. I greatly admired Janet, the owner of the preschool, and loved working with her.

One day Janet mentioned that she had to make a dessert for a meeting she was hosting at her house. I told her I had a delicious cheesecake recipe and I offered to make it for her. She gratefully took me up on my offer, and I made the cheesecake. It was a resounding success. Several women at the meeting asked for the recipe.

A few days later, as Janet and I sat in her home talking, in walked two of the women from the meeting. They asked if I had the recipe with me and I said no, that I didn't know they were going to be there that day. One of the women looked directly at me and said in a serious tone, "Well what good are you without your cheesecake recipe?" I was so taken aback that I couldn't even answer her!

I took the woman's question quite literally and the truth was...I didn't know. I didn't *know* what value I had without my cheesecake recipe.

I do not know what motivated the woman to ask me that question, but I spent the next 20 years of my life trying to come up with an answer. Time and time again I asked myself that same question—"What good *am* I without my cheesecake recipe?"

This question came to represent my search for self-worth. It was the question that surfaced each time I struggled to understand what good I was all by myself—independent of my children, my husband, and a job. Over the years I have come to realize that the cheesecake question was merely symbolic. The real question I was trying to answer was, "Who am I and what value do I have?"

a great deal of healing was needed

When I was asked the fateful "cheesecake question" I was 30 years old. I felt alone in the world despite having a husband, a child, family, and friends. I felt isolated. I carried emotional pain from earlier years: the suicide of my brother when I was in high school, the death of my mother when I was 22, a life-long strained and difficult relationship with my father, a deep sense of personal worthlessness.

The real issue that made all of these problems worse was that I didn't have the slightest idea how to heal them. I didn't *know* how to make myself feel better. Feelings of depression, self-loathing, and anger were my constant companions.

a journey of many steps

By the time I was 30 I was tired of feeling bad. I was tired of feeling disconnected from both the world and myself. I started taking steps to seek out help. I started reading books that taught me about healthier attitudes; I entered into therapy to explore the personal issues that caused me so much pain; I began to develop friendships with people who likewise deeply desired to grow.

Along the way it became apparent to me that the spiritual belief system I had grown up with was no longer a good fit. I began asking myself questions like, "Why was I born? Do I have a purpose on this earth? Why are any of us here?" As I explored these questions, I began to realize that the answers necessitated my being willing to examine my belief system. They challenged me to explore wider perspectives.

the origin of this book

I began the process of writing this book at age 48 when I received spiritual guidance to do so. I had never thought of myself as a writer and had no idea what it was Spirit wanted me to write about. I assumed that whatever I would be writing would be for my personal use only.

I started writing about the only subject that I knew intimately—my life. I began writing about my pain so that I might better understand it. I wrote about the steps I had taken toward healing and what I had learned in the process. I wrote about the activities that had been so vital to my emotional and spiritual growth. I included quotes, stories, and insights that had been of great value to me.

As I wrote, I gained more objectivity about both myself and my experiences. I also began to realize that there were many layers of pain that I had not yet addressed, so I set about working on them. As I wrote about the need for truth in our lives, I examined the areas of my own life where I was still being secretive. As I wrote about the need to *feel* in order to heal, I began to revisit the pain and shame of my brother's suicide. As I wrote about working with my Inner Child, I began to recognize the deep layers of hurt I continued to experience in my relationship with my father.

During the course of this lengthy process, it occurred to me that perhaps the writing I was doing would be beneficial to others as well. It was then that I began reorganizing the material into the book you are now holding.

walking the path

My path toward healing has not been short, nor has it been easy. It has, however, brought me a much deeper understanding of myself. I have come to understand that the real problems weren't my overeating or my feelings of low self-esteem but, rather, the silenced grief, anger, and hurt that gave birth to them. They were symptoms, not causes.

I am extremely grateful that I started on this path. While I believe personal growth is a life-long process that requires great courage and persistence, I have also found it to be deeply rewarding and immensely worthwhile. As I progress in this effort, my relationships—with both myself and others—have become more open, more loving, and more satisfying. I have also come to a much deeper understanding about God, the universe, and my place in it. I am beginning to understand who I *really* am.

If you are struggling with self-worth issues, know that you are not alone. Some of the brightest, most gifted people I know carry a sense of unworthiness within them. Viewing them from the outside, you would never surmise this. It is only when they are in an emotionally safe setting that they are free to acknowledge the sadness and pain they carry; the feelings of being defective.

These pages are an opportunity for me to share with others the lessons I am learning on my journey. It is my way of building a bridge to those who might also struggle with issues of self-worth, that they will know they are not alone. Come, dear one, take my hand. We can work on our healing together.

chapter 2

the early years

Sometimes, in order to understand ourselves in the present, we have to look back and understand ourselves in the past. When I was given the spiritual guidance to begin writing, I knew intuitively that I had to start at the beginning—to go back to the source of the emotional pain I have spent my life trying to heal. To do so, even after so much healing had taken place and so much time had passed, was not easy.

I was very surprised, as I wrote about my early years, at just how difficult a task it was. I had to pause from the writing, at times, to cry over the events that still brought up sadness. I was consciously revisiting issues that still held pain for me.

Why did I do it? Perhaps the best explanation lies in a story my friend Nolan once told me about a sailor, on a long voyage, who had cut his arm deeply. After a period of time the cut healed on the surface, but infection grew in its still unhealed bottom layers. Alone on the sailboat, without any medical help available, the sailor used a knife to reopen the wound and expose it to the air so that this time the bottom layers would heal as well.

It is my feeling that I was guided spiritually to reopen my emotional wounds so that, like the sailor, I could enable them to heal on a much deeper level. To help you better understand my journey, I share with you the sources of my pain.

early childhood

I was born into a devout Roman Catholic family, the fifth of six children. I had three older brothers and both an older and a younger sister. My parents were very hard-working people with deep religious beliefs and strong moral values. They had grown up on farms and had worked in the fields even as young children. Money had never come easily.

My mother was a full-time homemaker. She was quiet, very gentle, and loved children. I was comfortable with her and loved her deeply. Some of my fondest memories as a child are of times spent with my mother—doing needlework, baking cookies, writing out stacks and stacks of Christmas cards during the holidays. I have many cherished memories of coming home from school, sitting at the kitchen table, and telling my mother about my day.

My father and I did not share a similarly close relationship. He was very different in temperament from my mother. He was a salesman in a lumberyard and unhappy with his job. He was a very stern man and often angry.

Dad worked both a full-time and a part-time job to support the family, so he was frequently gone. When he was home, he was often impatient and frustrated with the clutter and demands of raising six children. I was glad that he worked so much. The atmosphere in our home was much more relaxed when he wasn't present.

As a very young child I loved my father and tried to think of ways to get his attention and approval, but I rarely felt successful. We seemed to have an emotional disconnection right from the start. I soon began to feel insignificant and of little value to him. As I got older and continued to feel unimportant and unacknowledged, I became resentful. During my teen years, I rebelled against my father's authoritarian ways. We had a very difficult, anger-filled relationship.

growing up in a large family

One of my parents' priorities was making sure that their children received Catholic educations, so they enrolled us in Catholic schools. My father worked long hours to be able to afford the tuition payments. My brothers and sisters and I attended religion classes every day at school for 12 years.

With six children, as would be expected, we had a very active household. Our home was not large—three bedrooms and only one bathroom—so we learned to share at a very young age. I had the typical relationships with my brothers and sisters; at times we were close and connected and, at other times, adversarial.

Because of my parents' greatly differing personalities, many of my siblings related much better to one parent than the other. I grew up with a sense of each of my parents "owning" certain children. Because my father and I had such a difficult relationship, my mother took me under her wing. I was clearly one of my mother's children.

There were distinct disadvantages and advantages growing up in a household of six children. We never had any privacy but we always had someone to play "tag" with outside after dark. We didn't have any closet space, but we did have someone to borrow clothes from. We had mounds of dirty dishes to wash after every meal, but there was always someone to dry them for you. There were times when I envied my friends who came from small families, and times when they envied me.

Some of my favorite memories are of things we did together as a family. We lived 35 miles from Lake Michigan and I loved going to the beach on hot, humid summer days. Some of my parents' friends had even larger families than we did, so when we got together at the lake, it was a lively time. We would swim, lie in the sun, and share a huge picnic lunch afterwards. I was one of the youngest and loved being around the older kids, whom I viewed with great admiration.

my brother Norman

One of the relationships that had a deep effect upon my life was with my brother, Norman. Norm was the first born in the family. He was 11 years older than me and lived away from home at a seminary each school year during most of my childhood. He had entered the seminary in ninth grade and spent the next 12 years studying to become a Catholic priest. We looked on Norm as the shining star of our family—extremely intelligent, fun loving, and full of life. He had a charismatic personality and we were all incredibly proud of him.

I recall, as a child, riding with my mother to St. Joseph's Seminary, which Norm attended, on Saturday mornings. It was a 30 minute ride each way and we would pick up Norm's dirty clothes and deliver clean clothing. He was not allowed to meet with us on those occasions, but I used to sweep the building with my eyes, hoping to catch a glimpse of him. He would include letters in the box of clothing he had left for us. It was always a great thrill to see a letter with *my* name on it.

The fact that Norm was gone most of the year gave him a celebrity status in my eyes when he came home on vacations. He often brought fellow students that lived out of town. As a young girl, I greatly admired Norm and his friends. I loved that these men were highly intelligent, compassionate, and sensitive. In ninth grade I made a conscious decision that the man I would marry would be an ex-seminarian.

As I became a teenager, Norm and I developed a closer relationship. We wrote long letters to each other and spent hours having conversations about spirituality. Norm thought "outside the box" and I was fascinated and challenged with the new concepts he spoke about. I had been deeply immersed in traditional religious concepts and I thoroughly enjoyed discussing his newer, more progressive ideas.

Norm continued his education at seminaries in Washington DC and Plymouth, Michigan. In the spring of 1965, a few weeks before he was to be ordained, he and I had a conversation in which he confided that he was questioning his choice to become a priest. He ultimately came to the conclusion that he would be suited to it, and was ordained a few weeks later. Norm had done what so many Catholic parents in the 1960s wished their son would do…he became a priest. It was an incredible honor for our family.

visiting my brother

I was a sophomore in high school when Norm was ordained. He was assigned to a parish in a small town about an hour and a half away from our home. During my junior year in high school I traveled by bus several times to visit him for the weekend. He had become friends with some of the parishioners, and one of the families, who had a teenage girl close to my age, generously allowed me to stay with them when I visited.

The summer before my senior year, Norm invited me to attend school in his town. He was frustrated with the conservative parish he had been placed in and told me how much he would welcome having a like-minded person around. He envisioned my assisting him on projects and I thought it sounded like fun. I viewed the idea as an adventure and, despite my parents' strong objections, I moved. I lived with a lovely family that Norm knew.

Once Norm and I started spending more time together, I began to understand just how frustrated he really was. His liberal views strongly conflicted with the conservative attitudes of his superiors. He felt lonely and very stifled. He questioned his decision to become a priest. He wished he had the freedom to marry and have a family of his own. He confided all these things in me and I swore I would not tell anyone.

I tried to assist in Norm's projects but it soon became apparent that our goals were not aligned. He wanted more of my time than I was willing to give. I was a senior in high school and wanted to date and have fun. He began to resent that.

At the same time, I started becoming concerned about the quality of the education I was receiving at my new school. It was significantly lower than what I was used to and I began to worry that it would negatively impact my getting into college. This concern, combined with my brother's disappointment in me, caused me to decide to move back home within just a matter of weeks.

coming back home

I readjusted easily to my former school. I became involved with studies and friends. I don't recall communicating with Norm in those busy weeks of readjustment. He had been busy as well. Soon after I left, he had been reassigned. He was sent to be the chaplain at a convent of cloistered nuns in a town farther north. It was as isolated an assignment as one could get.

We received a phone call the night before Thanksgiving telling us that Norm had been in a terrible automobile accident and was hospitalized. He had been driving along a country road when his car left the road and hit a tree. Norm hadn't been wearing a seatbelt. A nearby farmer pulled him out of the wreckage before the car caught fire. Norm was alive, but injured.

My mother, father, younger sister, and I made the three-hour trip to the hospital early the next morning. I remember feeling nauseous when I first saw Norm in the hospital. His face was black and blue from the impact. He couldn't talk to us; he had a broken jaw and the doctors had wired his jaws shut. We could see that he had teeth missing. It didn't even look like Norm, his face was so swollen.

I don't know if Norm had other injuries. All I can remember is the sight of his face. I do recall someone asking us if we wanted to get something to eat; that they were serving Thanksgiving dinner down in the cafeteria. My stomach turned at the very thought of it.

the recuperation period

When Norm was released from the hospital, he came home to stay with us. My mother nursed him back to health. She prepared nutritious beverages that he sipped through a straw. He couldn't open his mouth because his jaws were still wired shut. He couldn't talk.

I was incredibly uncomfortable around him. I was afraid that he was still upset with me for disappointing him. I felt horrible about this terrible accident and the pain he was experiencing. He was sullen and kept to himself. I busied myself with school activities and friends.

By late winter Norm had healed enough to be able to resume his responsibilities at the convent. My mother and sister went up once to visit him but I didn't go.

complete disbelief

The morning of May 16, 1967, I was sitting in an English class when someone knocked on the classroom door. My teacher opened the door and spoke briefly with the person in the hall. He then turned and said quietly, "Virginia, you are wanted at the office." I immediately knew something was amiss. We were *never* excused from classes in this fashion. As I walked past my teacher we both paused for just a moment. I could tell by the compassionate look in his eyes that something was terribly wrong.

As soon as I stepped into the hallway I could see my sister-in-law standing by the office door, waiting for me. I rushed to her and asked what had happened. Reluctantly she replied, "It's Norm. He's dead." She slowly proceeded, "He killed himself."

In a state of total numbness, I went with her to our house. My family members were outside, standing around the picnic table. I struggled to grasp the information I was being given about my brother. He had asphyxiated himself. It didn't seem possible to me that Norm was dead; he was only 28 years old. To say our family was shocked would be a *vast* understatement.

I was told not to tell anyone that Norm had killed himself. We were to tell others that he had died as a result of his previous automobile accident.

The events of the next few days, including the funeral, are a blur to me. I remember my father, sitting in his chair, blankly staring forward for long periods of time. I remember there being an issue of whether or not Norm would be allowed to be buried in a Catholic cemetery because of having committed suicide. I remember agonizing over the thought that my beloved brother could possibly spend all eternity in Hell.

living with the guilt

I don't know when the guilt started to surface, only that it did. I believed that Norm's suicide was *my* fault; that I could have prevented it. I had been the family member that had known how frustrated he was; how lonely and troubled. I felt terribly responsible. I told myself that not only had I not recognized the severity of his unhappiness, I had **added** to it by being such a disappointment to him.

I didn't feel free to discuss Norm's death with anyone. I didn't want them to hate me, as I hated myself, for causing his death. I buried the pain and guilt within myself.

We didn't really talk much about Norm after that, even to each other. We just dealt with it individually as best we could. We didn't tell people the real cause of his death because of the tremendous stigma attached to suicide. The fact that Norm, a deeply religious priest, and larger-than-life person, had committed suicide was absolutely unbelievable to us.

Two weeks after we buried my brother, I graduated high school. My mother held a graduation open house for me. In hindsight, I'm not sure how my mother ever gathered the strength to carry on and celebrate my graduation. I suspect things seemed as surreal to the rest of my family as they did to me; we were going through the motions of resuming a normal life knowing, all the time, that things would *never* be normal again.

Several years later, one of my brothers asked if I had ever considered the possibility that Norm's automobile accident had been a suicide attempt. I vehemently dismissed the idea at first. After thinking about it later, however, and rethinking the circumstances of the accident, I sadly came to the conclusion that he was correct.

continuing on

The fall after Norm died, I became a full-time student at our local community college. The rest of my siblings carried on with their lives as well: my older brothers and sister working full-time, my younger sister entering her sophomore year in high school.

In January of my freshman year in college, my mother asked a favor of me—to show Tom Sobel, the son of her friend, around the school. Tom had attended a seminary during his high school years and had recently made the decision to leave the seminary. I knew Tom, as we had attended the same elementary school. In fact, we had been in the same classroom all eight years.

I agreed to give Tom a tour of the college and we discovered we shared common interests—playing guitar and singing. Soon after, we joined two other friends in creating a folk group. We began playing guitars and singing weekly at progressive "guitar masses." We went on to play at Christmas parties, art shows, and other functions. Being in this group brought me a great deal of joy.

Tom and I began to spend more and more time together. Within a few months we realized that what we felt was something more than friendship. We began dating the fall of my sophomore year. Three years later, we would marry. I kept my ninth grade promise to myself—I was marrying an ex-seminarian.

in the meantime

During the three years Tom and I dated, we were both very busy. We finished our studies at the community college. Tom went on to a university while I took a year off to work full-time and travel. After the year was up I resumed my studies, majoring in elementary education.

The summer before we were married, Tom's 53-year-old father died of congestive heart failure. Wally was a kind and gentle man and it was a very difficult time for Tom's family. I had gotten to know Wally in the recent years, and his death left me deeply saddened. It also added to the feelings of grief I had been trying to deal with in the three years since my brother died.

our first year of marriage

The following summer, in 1971, one week after Tom graduated college, we were married. We spent the summer in married housing at the university I attended. In the fall, we moved back to the city in which we were raised, and I began to teach. The college program I was enrolled in required year-round classes and enabled its participants to assume full teaching responsibilities in a classroom their senior year.

My first year of marriage was a flurry of activity. I had been given a challenging assignment as a kindergarten teacher in two different schools. It meant double of everything: two classrooms to prepare; two sets of staff to familiarize myself with; double the staff meetings. The schools were several miles apart, so every day at noon I would load up my teaching materials and travel from one school to the next.

I don't remember seeing my family much those first few months. I was overwhelmed with my teaching responsibilities and busy trying to adjust to being married. I do remember my mother having an x-ray taken in the fall. She was never one to complain and I found out about it from a third party. I remember being very upset with her for not telling me, but she assured me she was fine.

a routine procedure

In March of that school year my mother told me that she was scheduled for minor surgery at our local Catholic hospital. The surgery was scheduled for a Saturday morning. I vividly remember, during her surgery, sitting in a waiting area near a bank of elevators with my father, younger sister, and one of my brothers.

After what seemed like a long time, my mother's surgeon stepped off the elevator. He approached us in a very serious manner, and said, "I'm sorry to tell you that she is full of cancer. We opened her up but couldn't do anything so we closed her right back up."

We all just stood there in disbelief. I remember the deep shock and horror I felt. My mind raced—this couldn't possibly be happening to *my* mother. I don't recall anything else until later that afternoon when I went home to our apartment to tell Tom.

Tom and I went for a long walk. I cried. I just kept thinking, "This can't possibly be true. I can't get along without her." I was 22 years old and not ready to let go of my mother. I begged and begged God to let her live.

the second surgery

It was decided that we should not tell mom about the cancer, so we kept it a secret. I remember visiting her after the surgery, trying to make light conversation. It was incredibly difficult, given the situation. All I really wanted to do was to break down and cry.

The doctor thought that my mother should have a second surgery to see if the cancer could be removed, so one week after the initial surgery she was again operated on. The surgeon found that there was nothing he could do. The cancer had progressed too far.

A few days later we received conflicting information. We were given incredibly good news—that the type of cancer my mother had was slow growing; that she would live for some time to come. (I took that to mean a number of years.) We all breathed a sigh of relief; we had been given a reprieve.

I felt as though a huge weight had been taken from my shoulders. I had always been conscious of my deep love for my mother; now I would have more time to show her.

She was released from the hospital and sent home to recuperate from the surgeries. My younger sister, Marlene, who was living at home at the time, took care of my mother, because I needed to go back to my classrooms.

The following Saturday morning Marlene called me and said, "You need to come over right away. Mom's not doing well. I'm worried." I went to the house and saw my mother in such a weakened state that she couldn't even stand by herself. I knew we had to take her back to the hospital.

Because of her prognosis, I was sure that this was only a temporary setback. She was fearful of going back into the hospital so I assured her as she lay on her bed that she would be okay. I *promised* her that I would bring her back home. The fact that I couldn't keep that promise would haunt me for years.

keeping vigil

Once we readmitted mom to the hospital and tests were run, we were told that there was no hope for her recovery. The cancer was rampant. We were devastated.

Mother's health began to deteriorate more and more as each day passed. Within a week we realized that death was not far away. We took turns staying by her bed so that she would have family members with her 24 hours a day.

I can't express the pain I felt watching cancer ravage my beloved mother's body. I remember keeping vigil with my aunt one particular night. It was about 3:00 am and the room was dark. She and I sat, staring out a window at the streetlights in the distance. As we watched cars go by, I remember thinking, "How is it possible that life is still going on for these people? Don't they know that our world is coming to an end?"

Toward the end of my mother's life she started going in and out of a coma-like state. She awoke from it one afternoon and told me that her father and Norm were waiting for her to join them. At the time I wondered if she was hallucinating. Now I believe they really were there to guide her transition.

She died soon after. She was 59 years old. It had been four weeks since her initial surgery.

chapter 3

coping with the grief

I graduated college in June of 1972, just a few weeks after my mother died. I remember feeling as though I was in a fog the day of commencement. What was supposed to be one of the proudest days of my life felt flat and painful.

Following my graduation, Tom and I moved across the state so he could attend law school. For the next three years I taught elementary school while Tom was a full-time student. I was miserably unhappy during those three years and didn't like being in the classroom. My grief robbed me of the energy that teaching demanded. I also didn't like being so far away from most of my family.

I began to feel depressed and started having thoughts of suicide. I was frightened by the belief that I was somehow genetically predisposed to suicide because Norm had made that choice. Prior to Norm's death, I had never given much thought to the act of suicide. I had never before been touched by it. Now that I had, I felt much more vulnerable—as though it was an option.

On my way to school in the morning I would think about how I could kill myself and have it look like an accident so my family wouldn't be further burdened by a second suicide. My grief had become all encompassing. I just wanted to be released from the emotional pain I felt almost constantly.

It's sad to me now I didn't realize that my death—no matter what the circumstances—would have been devastating to my husband and family. I just didn't know that I mattered.

In our apartment, after school, I would eat to push down the overwhelming feelings I was experiencing—feelings of grief, of guilt, of despair. The worse I felt, the more I isolated myself and ate. I began to put on weight and, as I did, I became even more depressed.

I felt so very lost without my mother. She had been my emotional base and I didn't know how to cope with all the pain I felt. I had no idea how to heal the hole in my heart that her leaving caused. I couldn't imagine ever feeling better.

silenced grief

A large regret that I have about those early years is that I didn't seek professional help. I desperately needed someone to help me understand the emotional turmoil that I was experiencing. It was the 1970s, though, and there was a great stigma attached to being in therapy. I don't even remember considering it as an option.

For the most part, I struggled with my internal chaos alone. I had grown up in an environment of secrecy—of keeping things to oneself— so that was what I did. When I went to visit my father, we never mentioned either my mother or my brother. It was as though they had never existed.

The depression I experienced left me with a feeling of emotional numbness. Everything in my life at that time felt like an incredible burden. I felt drained both emotionally and physically. I hated myself and I hated my situation. At night I would lie in bed and literally have anxiety attacks. My heart would race and I would feel panicky. I would think about my life—how bad everything was and how defective I was.

I spoke with my siblings about my grief at times, but never told them about the responsibility I felt I bore for Norm's death. I didn't want them to hate me. One of my sisters lived in the same city I was living in. I never once told her I had thoughts of suicide. I didn't want to add to the burden of grief she already carried.

I also never told Tom about my depression and thoughts of suicide. He was coping with the rigors of law school and the grief he and his family were experiencing because of his father's death. We didn't turn to each other in our losses; we didn't know how.

The fact that my family and I had lied about the cause of Norm's death further distanced me from receiving the help from others that I so desperately needed. I didn't talk about Norm with friends because they might ask questions about the circumstances surrounding his death. My mother hadn't even told most of her sisters and brothers, whom she loved dearly, that Norm's death was a suicide. The lie didn't protect us; it created a barrier to the support that we needed so badly.

lifelines

Looking back now, I realize that there were two lifelines that were thrown to me during this time when I was in such need of them. The first came in the way of a sympathetic friend, the second in the form of writing. Each of them provided a means for me to begin expressing what I was holding so deeply within.

My first lifeline appeared while I was teaching. I became acquainted with one of the other elementary teachers, Kaye Keller. She was very friendly and started coming to my classroom after school each day, visiting for a few minutes. After a while, we began to eat lunch together in my classroom, instead of the teachers' lounge. She encouraged me to talk and I started to open up to her. It was difficult for me, but I felt very safe with her.

As our friendship deepened, I began to tell Kaye about my depression and how I was afraid that it meant I was faulty. I told her the great amount of shame and grief I felt. I also told her about the suicidal thoughts I entertained on my hour commute to school each day.

Kaye listened with compassion and sensitivity. She didn't judge me, even though I judged myself harshly. Instead, she just patiently showed up at my classroom door day after day. She soon began urging me to tell Tom how I felt, and although it was difficult, I did. He was so concerned that he barely let me out of his sight for the next few days.

Opening up to Kaye was my first step toward healing. Looking back, I realize how incredibly blessed I was by this gentle woman's compassion. I have no idea how she knew I was in such pain, or why she cared so much, but I will be forever grateful. She was an angel in my life when I needed one most.

giving words to my feelings

A second lifeline that was extended to me came in the form of a class I had previously taken in college. In this particular English class, we were required to keep a semester-long journal. In the journal, we were to write entries that described our thoughts and feelings.

During this class, I had found the process to be helpful and quite different from the diaries I had kept as a child. In my diaries I had recorded events and activities. My college journal entries were much more subjective, often filled with emotion, and much more self-revealing.

I decided to begin this process of journaling again. I purchased a small book with lined pages. It had a red and blue Asian motif and felt very nurturing to me. In it, I began to write about my life and my feelings.

I found that it soon began to act as a "safety valve" for me. When I felt overwhelmed I would turn to it as one would turn to a friend. I could write down what I was thinking or feeling, without worrying that someone else would judge me. It helped me to cope.

It was the first of many journals I would buy in the years to come.

journal entries

During the course of the next few years I wrote many journal entries. I have decided to include some of those entries here because I feel they best chronicle that time in my life. I have placed the journal entries in italics for the sake of clarity.

As I reread the following entry, I remember so clearly the pain that I felt at being motherless in my early 20s. I had an emotionally distant relationship with my father, so my mother's death left me with a feeling of being literally orphaned. I ached for her gentle hug, her loving concern, her assurance that I was deeply loved. I missed her terribly and felt helpless at not having been able to make her well.

September 12, 1973

(**My sister**) *Shirley and I spent the evening sorting through recipes and dishes of Mom's tonight. It was really depressing. We didn't want to throw anything away because everything was a part of her. It's as though they are an extension of Mom. I wanted to scream or cry or something. Just yell "Damn it. I don't want these. I want Mom!"*

Grief is so damned frustrating. It's so personal. I miss her. I feel like a little kid. I want my mom. Just when I was getting old enough to do things for her, I can't. She helped me so many times and yet when it came down to the line—to her being sick—there wasn't anything I could do. I couldn't come through.

I just felt a need to write tonight. I don't know what for. I feel so mixed up sometimes. Maybe by putting things down on paper I will be able to understand myself better. I think I've got a long way to go.

Oftentimes, a complex mixture of grief, guilt, and anger overwhelmed me. I used journaling as a means of coping. Journaling was a way of expressing myself—of getting the emotions "outside of myself." The process helped release some of the intensity of my feelings.

May 10, 1975

I need a sounding board tonight and you're the most available. I really feel like I am going over the brink. Like I am slowly, slowly falling into a darkness where I won't have any control over my emotions. Sometimes there is a war raging within me. It is such a battle to contain the bubbling emotions. I get so frustrated I want to scream or cry or both.

When I came to bed tonight, Tom kiddingly said he thought I was going to make it. Sometimes I'm not so sure of that.

In many of my journal entries I mentioned my weight and the self-contempt I had because of it. As I look back now, I realize that in putting so much emphasis on my weight I was focusing on a symptom—not the problem. My problem was the deep grief, depression, and guilt I felt.

I am amazed as I look back over these older journal entries that I never once wrote about the tremendous guilt I felt over my brother's suicide and rarely wrote about the devastation I felt when my mother died. I also didn't address the impact these deaths had on my belief in God. I had a strong faith prior to these experiences. My faith in God was totally shaken as I watched my mother's body be ravaged by cancer.

It took me years to realize that I developed an unconscious belief about my own body as I watched my mother suffer: that you couldn't trust your body. It caused me to have a love/hate relationship with my own body for the next 25 years.

May 22, 1975

My weight has been a horrible, nagging problem to me (especially lately it seems). I can't reconcile myself to staying heavy like this, and buying new clothes would be an acceptance of the permanence of it. I just can't do that.

I keep telling myself that it would be a waste to buy size 16–18 clothes because they'd all go to waste after I lose my weight. The only problem is that I keep gaining—not losing. I am down to such a pitifully small wardrobe. Sometimes I get so frustrated by it, I could almost cry. And then—out of frustration—I eat. I just can't seem to get on top of this problem.

In June of 1975 Tom graduated law school and accepted a position as an associate with a law firm in a small town along Lake Michigan. We were once again closer to home. It was a luxury being less than an hour's drive from our families.

Within a few months I became pregnant, and in 1976 our daughter Amanda was born. The joy of her birth triggered a fresh wave of grief over my mother's death that was as intense as when my mother first died. It was deeply painful not to be able to share this incredible new experience with my mother.

In hindsight, I now realize that I, myself, was deeply in need of mothering. I was living in a new city, a full-time homemaker, and terribly lonely. I knew only the people who worked with my husband. Tom worked long hours and I felt isolated and often terribly insecure about my ability to be a good parent. I remember thinking, "This is how Eve must have felt with her first child…so alone."

February 7, 1977

I have really come to love Amanda. I try very, very hard to be a good mother to her. I want to give her so much—I want to fill her to the brim with love and self-confidence. I want her to know that she is capable of doing anything she really sets her mind to do. I want her to like herself. (That more than anything.)

Because of my own insecurities, I am constantly plagued with doubts about how to raise her, take care of her, feed her, meet her needs, etc. It's a constantly changing, demanding, challenging situation. I want so badly to do well.

February 22, 1977
I read an article recently about depression and very much identified with it. The article really opened my eyes. I had been aware of the symptoms (sadness, lethargy, and putting on weight); but didn't really come face to face with the problem. I am facing it now and am taking positive steps to overcome it. I think I am heading in the right direction. I am starting to become more of the person that I want to be.

During this time, Tom and I began taking classes on spirituality at the Catholic church we attended. They were stimulating and I enjoyed them immensely. They gave me a change of scenery, a relinquishing (at least for short periods of time) of Mandy's care, an opportunity to meet new people, and thought-provoking discussions. The topics that were raised in the classes caused me to stand back and take a more objective look at my life.

September 15, 1977
My life as it really is? It is so very hard to summarize. Like anyone's life—a combination of good and bad. The good: Mandy—I love her very, very much; Thomas; our new home. The bad: The incredible boredom of being home all the time; feeling guilty if Mandy has a hard time when I do go away. Mandy's dependence can seem overwhelming at times.

I am deeply involved in a search for my own identity and self-worth. I have an awfully long way to go. I progress, I regress, I get depressed. I guess I do feel very passive in my world—as though I have so little affect upon it. How to have more affect?

Around this time, I became friends with a woman in whom I felt comfortable confiding. As I told her about my past experiences and the unresolved emotions I carried, she encouraged me to go into therapy. She said she had been in therapy and it had helped her greatly. Soon after, I began to see a counselor, Nina.

August 14, 1978

I get so frustrated with myself at times. When I look at my life objectively it seems a person in my situation would be extremely happy—a new house, a husband with a good career, a beautiful 2-year-old daughter. All my goals realized. All the things I dreamed of—my tickets to happiness. Isn't it ironic, then, that here I sit frustrated and unhappy?

I feel no one is a greater mystery to me than I am to myself. I am not content with the person that I am now. In fact, I would say I very much dislike myself.

I have been in counseling since March. I have come to have tremendous respect for Nina. I wonder how it must feel to be a therapist. She seems so emotionally healthy. I envy her and wonder if I could ever possibly be that secure and self-confident.

I wonder what she is thinking as I talk to her—I worry about her being impatient with my slow progress. Maybe if I knew more of the problem, I could find more of the answer. I find it so difficult to know myself—how I am feeling, what it is that I want, why I am unhappy.

Things seem so much simpler and more logical when I talk with Nina—so easy to rectify. Habits don't seem nearly so hard to break and at times I can even see the light at the end of the tunnel. It's been four weeks now since I've had an appointment, though, and that light seems to be farther and farther away.

As I struggled with my inner turmoil and the demands of being a full-time mother, I often found myself eating out of frustration. Then, when I put on weight, my insecurities would heighten and I would isolate myself further. I was painfully self-conscious and fearful of the judgment of others. It was a vicious cycle. On several occasions I had experiences, like the following, that reinforced my feelings of self-loathing.

December 2, 1978

Tom and I went out to eat tonight with another couple. Because of my weight and lack of anything to wear, I am getting to dread such occasions. I really psyched myself up tonight, though, and decided I'd have a good time.

While the four of us were waiting for our suppers to arrive, a man passed by our table and said hi quite loudly to Tom. On his way back he stopped to talk to us. I didn't recall ever having seen the man before. In a loud voice he looked at me, tapped my shoulder and said, "You're getting to look just like me..." and patted his protruding stomach. He continued to say that I had put on a lot of weight.

Oh, if I could have just disappeared!! I was so embarrassed! The next few minutes were so uncomfortable for everyone at the table. I—and everyone else—tried to pretend that nothing had happened.

Here we were, all thinking about what had just taken place and no one talking about it. I was so upset the rest of the meal and tried valiantly to hide it.

Because I thought I was "defective," and didn't want other people to likewise discover that about me, I adopted the persona of someone who was cheerful and happy. I would smile and try to act easy-going so that people wouldn't see the incredible sense of emotional heaviness that I carried within.

I was very frightened that people would leave me if they knew who I really was, so I projected an image of the person I thought they wanted to see. Occasionally, someone would be able to see past my persona. When they did, it made me extremely uncomfortable.

December 6, 1979

*I had such an interesting evening tonight. (Why is it whenever I have an evening I wouldn't want to repeat I term it **interesting**?) I went to a Christmas supper for the Young Mothers Group. It went just fine until I realized I was going to end up sitting next to Diana.*

I did just fine for about 20 minutes because we talked about her and her family during that time. The conversation turned to me eventually, as I knew it would, and I became more and more uncomfortable.

I don't like to be around Diana because I think she gets right to the heart of me. I believe she knows I am unhappy with myself; terribly uptight about being overweight; feeling bored and depressed; feeling as though I am not growing as a person. I truly believe she senses these things within me. I squirm so when Diana pokes into the true me—I can't get away with putting on a happy act around her.

Going into therapy was very beneficial because it helped me to gain more objectivity about myself. I wasn't yet ready at that time, though, to tackle the deeper emotional issues that held so much pain for me.

One of the issues I was aware of was my repressed anger. I remember having a conversation with a friend in which I told her, "I *never* let my anger out because it could hurt someone." I described it to her as a tiger that I held inside. I didn't have the slightest idea how to express anger in a healthy manner so I didn't express it at all. I just pushed it all down.

January 21, 1980
I feel so uptight; so aggressive; so explosive. I can't really label these feelings within me and that frustrates me even more. I want to lash out—to fight—but I don't know with whom or why.

March 9, 1980
*I went out to dinner with (**my friend**) Sue and her mother tonight and I feel so sad now. I really am glad that Sue has her mom here but yet it really hurts at times. They are so close; they share so much; they love each other so.*

When we walked out of the restaurant tonight it was a bit slippery and I found myself starting to repeat an action I haven't done in nine years…I started to hold my arm out (just as I always did for my mom) so Sue's mother could steady herself on the ice. The action was immediate—almost second nature to me. Perhaps for a second I thought it was Mom and not Mrs. G. When the reality of the situation occurred to me, it saddened me instantly.

I went home that night and did what I had never done before—I allowed myself to express the anger I felt over my mother's death. I lay on my bed, hitting the mattress and screaming into a pillow. I wrote about the experience afterwards in my journal:

> I miss you so much, Mother, and I am angry that you left me. Do you know how unfair it all is? Do you know I am practically the only one I know without a mother? Is it fair, God, that I be so shortchanged? Is it fair that I will never again be loved as Sue is loved? Oh, God, there are so many millions and billions of things I want to share with Mom.
>
> I do hate you, Mother, for leaving us. I hate you, and I love you, and I miss you terribly all rolled up together.
>
> Mandy has been so cheated. Not just a little bit…a huge amount. Mother, how can you not know the most important person in my life right now? Oh, Mother, how I want to share her with you. I am not a little girl anymore. I am a mother. And I ache to share that with you. God—how could you cheat me out of that??

Even though it was emotionally painful going through the experience that night, I am very grateful for it. I understand now that it was a necessary step in my grieving process. Prior to that evening, whenever the anger toward my mother came up, I had intellectualized it away. I would think, "What sense does it make for me to be mad at Mom? Do I really think that she **wanted** to die a painful death?" I would then shove the feelings of anger down.

I know now that anger is a very natural part of the grieving process. I had not previously acknowledged the anger I felt at my mother's leaving me. I took a huge step forward that night in the grieving process. It was a significant step in my starting to release the "tiger" I had in my stomach.

chapter 4

choosing to heal

Several of my friends had trouble turning 30. It symbolized to them a loss of their youth; an entering into a less carefree, "adult" stage of life. I felt completely different. I not only didn't mind turning 30, I was actually pleased to be doing so. I was anxious to leave behind the difficulty and turmoil that I had experienced in my earlier years. I desperately wanted a change; I desperately wanted things to improve.

By the time I was in my late 20s, I had begun to realize that if things were ever going to get better in my life, it would be up to me to make that happen. Even though I felt a great deal of distance between a Higher Power and myself, I began by asking God daily for help. I also began by reaching out to others.

By the time I was 30, I could see that I was starting to make progress in my life. I was beginning to release some of the terrible emotional heaviness that I had carried around for so many years.

the intention to heal

I think that the intention to heal is a powerful thing. It literally changes one's life path. I made the decision to heal in my late 20s out of self-preservation. It was really very simple…I just wanted to feel better. I needed to feel better. I didn't want to go through the rest of my life feeling so emotionally burdened.

Unsure of how to go about making myself feel better, I started looking to outside sources. One of the steps I took was to seek out professional help through counseling. With a therapist's objectivity and assistance I was able to identify many of the attitudes and issues that needed to be examined in my life. I began to realize that just because I had been taught something as a child didn't mean that it was emotionally healthy.

I also began to consciously develop friendships with people who were likewise interested in personal growth. I wanted people around me who would support my healthy changes and who would lovingly challenge me when they thought I wasn't being honest with myself. One friend in particular, Tena, and I, spent numerous hours discussing new concepts and whether or not they were applicable to our lives. We encouraged each other in the steps we were taking and worked on issues that surfaced in our own relationship.

Another step I took was to seek the guidance of professionals through books. I gravitated to empowering books that gave me insights into healthier attitudes. In my 30s I particularly liked the writings of Louise L. Hay, Dr. Wayne Dyer, and David D. Burns, M.D. I have read numerous books over the last 25 years and am very grateful for the inspiration they have given me.

I also began to address my relationship with God. I started to examine the religious beliefs that I grew up with and found that I was feeling increasingly out of sync with them, so I started exploring other spiritual concepts. This process was especially difficult for me since my family held such strong beliefs in Catholicism.

One of the bravest steps I took initially on my healing path was to attend a weeklong metaphysical retreat. The retreat was non-denominational and sought to explore universal truths. Attending this retreat has become an annual tradition for me. It has been a source of deep healing.

Setting an intention to heal motivated me to be open to other sources of insight as well. I began to seek out classes that pertained to personal growth and spiritual seeking. Some of these classes lasted an evening, some lasted several weeks, and some evolved into ongoing groups that lasted for several years. All of them were instrumental in opening up my awareness to the larger world around me.

learning to communicate

In hindsight, one of the most important lessons I learned through my healing process was the importance of building bridges of communication to others: to friends, family, counselors, and, perhaps most importantly of all, a Higher Power. As I did so, I began to understand that my perception of the world had been inaccurate. I *wasn't* defective because of the emotional turmoil that I experienced within.

Bit by bit, I began to address my pain instead of isolating myself because of it. I worked on being honest with my siblings, my friends, and my therapist even when I felt great fear that they would judge me for my anger and depression. I began to understand that in order to release my feelings of grief over the deaths of my mother and brother, I needed to talk about them.

I spoke about my childhood and gradually gained more insight into the relationship between my father and myself. I began to see how the unexpressed anger I felt toward my father had turned inward, causing me to become depressed. I began to understand the tremendous toll that secrecy about Norm's death had taken on me. I started gaining an objectivity that I greatly needed.

I found that when I opened myself up with deep honesty, I wasn't rejected by the other person. In fact, I found the opposite to be true. I found my relationships deepening. Being honest with family and friends about my vulnerabilities created a safe space for them to talk about their own. I grew to appreciate a deeper level of emotional intimacy in my relationships.

a huge step forward

Much of my progress has been made in tiny baby steps. There are particular experiences, however, that stand out in my mind as moving me forward much more quickly.

The evening spent with my friend, Sue, and her mother was one of those experiences. When I felt the loss of my own mother that evening, I was, for the first time, able to express the anger that I felt over her leaving. It was a profoundly healing step for me to take. I learned a great lesson that evening about the importance of honoring *all* of the feelings that we experience during grief…whether or not they make sense to us.

Another deeply healing step took place during a conversation with my older sister, Shirley. When I was 29, 12 years after our brother Norm died, we had a late night, heart-to-heart conversation in which I confessed a long held secret—that it was *my* fault that Norm had committed suicide.

As I cried, I told her that since I had lived in the same city with him, and been very close to him, I should have seen the emotional pain he was in. I went on to tell her how I had disappointed him and felt I had made everything worse.

Shirley looked at me and said with deep sincerity, "No, it is *my* fault. I was so wrapped up with my own life that I didn't spend enough time with him." I was completely taken aback by her statement. It took a few moments for me to process what she was saying. I had no idea that she had felt that way!

As I sat there in complete surprise, I began to think, "How was it possible that we *both* felt solely responsible? How could we *each* have carried such a heavy burden of guilt for all those years?" In that instant

I knew that it wasn't my sister's fault that Norm had chosen to commit suicide. And if *that* was true, maybe it wasn't my fault either.

Both Shirley and I took a large step toward healing that day. In the years since then, we have had many conversations about the tremendous legacy of guilt that Norm's suicide left behind. Slowly we have begun to realize that we were not responsible for his death.

the challenge of change

In addition to addressing painful emotional issues, my healing process has entailed learning and adopting many new attitudes. I needed to learn new patterns to replace the self-destructive patterns I previously held. I learned that I need to love and nurture myself; that honest communication enhances, not harms, a relationship; and that we are ultimately responsible for the way we experience our lives.

Adopting these new attitudes, and many others, has been a long, slow process for me. Sometimes I struggled to understand the concepts intellectually because they were so vastly different from anything I had ever learned. More often, the real challenge would lie in staying mindful of the new attitudes and applying them to my life on a consistent basis.

I have found the process of healing to come in an irregular path rather than a straight line. Often I have taken two steps forward, then one step back. It has usually taken great effort to consciously put a new idea into practice. It is significantly easier to resort back to my old "default" settings. Choosing to incorporate new attitudes has taken both persistence and courage, but the results have been well worth the effort.

the larger picture

The choice to heal is one that takes a great deal of courage. It is my observation that many people never choose to do so because of the fear it brings up in them. I can understand that. I know the fear. I have lived with that fear. The challenge is to not let it stop us.

Growth is an ongoing process that requires a great deal of persistence. In my life it has involved literally thousands of small baby steps and a few giant leaps. Perhaps, more than anything, it requires determination.

I have found, though, that the effort is rewarded. It *does* make a difference. It *does* change your life. I am grateful for every experience I've had; every small step of progress I've made. I can truthfully tell you that I am not the same person I would have been had I not chosen this path.

As I have made progress in my life I have learned that I *am* capable of perceiving my world differently. I am not destined to think what I thought yesterday; I am not destined to remain emotionally in the same spot. I can change. We *all* can. We all have that innate ability. It is up to us. It is a choice that we make.

chapter 5

a larger perspective

I'm the **best** me I've ever been. I'm not all of what I want to be, but thank God I'm not what I used to be.

John Lucas

When I first heard John Lucas make the above statement I thought, "That's it! That's *exactly* how I feel!" I'm not all of what I want to be. Some days I feel very centered and "on track." Other days, when new challenges present themselves, I may not even feel very close to getting where I want to be. At those times it is especially important for me to remember how things *used* to be and how I *used* to feel. When I do, I am filled with a deep sense of gratitude. I have come a great distance.

I have found that learning my life lessons does not prevent me from going through difficult times. We are, after all, works in progress. I consciously practice applying the principles I have learned, but there are times when I become forgetful. The challenge for me, then, is to recognize my lapse as soon as I can and try to learn what I can from the experience.

I once heard the growth process described in the following way: "The process of living is like walking up a hill. Periodically we encounter challenges that cause us to lose our footing and tumble back down. Prior to making changes in our lives, we may tumble all the way to the bottom, perhaps remaining there for a long time. If, however, we have prepared ourselves for the trip up the hill by gaining new insights, when we do fall we will either grab onto a branch on our way down, or, if we do tumble all the way down, spend less time at the bottom. Either way, we will be back on our path to well-being much more quickly. Staying at the bottom of the hill won't become a way of life."

examining my beliefs

In my desire to move uphill, I knew that I needed to give serious thought as to what I believed spiritually. My belief in God had been an important part of my early years, yet in my 20s all I felt was a great separation from Him. I felt a great deal of anger toward God, but was frightened to acknowledge that—even to myself.

I have spent the last 25 years examining my spiritual beliefs. I began by deeply questioning where my mother and brother went after they died and whether or not they continued to exist at all. I repeatedly questioned the purpose of life and why I was on earth. I allowed myself to question the existence of God and, if there *was* a God, why it was that He allowed suffering and pain. I frequently thought, "What is this all about?"

I found myself gravitating toward metaphysics. Metaphysics addressed the questions for which I needed answers. Perhaps the clearest definition of metaphysics that I have found is from the book *The New Dictionary of Spiritual Thought* by Carol Parrish-Harrah. In it, she describes metaphysics as "The study of laws higher than the physical and dealing with universal truths to teach humanity to align with the purpose and plan of life."

The process I went through was very unsettling at first. I felt as though I was taking all of my lifelong spiritual beliefs and throwing them up into the air. One by one, over the years, I pulled each of them down and decided whether or not I still believed it. The fact that I had been taught something as a child wasn't sufficient now. I needed to consciously choose for myself. Some of my childhood beliefs still held great meaning for me after this examining process; many did not.

choosing a different path

As a child, belonging to an organized religion was a way of life for me. I now view spirituality very differently. I no longer see spirituality as being dependent upon a church, or a priest, or a minister, or a prescribed belief system. I see it as being much simpler and far more direct than that—it is our relationship with both God and with ourselves.

We are each unique beings. For some, belonging to an organized religion is a wonderful path toward spirituality and a deeper awareness of their Higher Power. There is often great support and encouragement within a congregation. That path does not suit everyone, however. Some people find that the dogma of organized religion inhibits, rather than encourages, the development of their spirituality.

I am embarrassed now by the arrogance I felt growing up. I looked at anyone who left the Catholic church as a "fallen away" Catholic. It never once occurred to me that someone might actually *choose* to separate themselves from organized religion because they were following a different path. It never occurred to me that they might, in fact, be a "walked away" Catholic.

I have now come to realize that a person's choice to attend—or not attend—church is not an indicator of the depth of their spiritual convictions. The indicator lies in the degree to which a person has undertaken a conscious path toward discovering what they truly believe. The indicator lies in whether or not their actions are in harmony with their beliefs. My convictions are far more meaningful to me now than they were when I was merely accepting other people's beliefs without questioning them for myself.

I have made many changes in my attitudes and beliefs over the years. I have come to realize that each of us has a highly individualized path to God. Just as there is more than one way to get from New York to Los Angeles, there is more than one way to become aware of our innate connection to our Creator.

the importance of our spiritual beliefs

It is important for us to recognize the spiritual beliefs that we hold because they have a profound impact upon our lives. They are literally our framework for interpreting the world around us. A person's core spiritual beliefs deeply affect the way they perceive both themselves and others.

I have come to recognize a great connection between what I believe spiritually and how I interpret my experiences. The manner in which I interpret my experiences will then affect how I feel about them. As I have shifted my beliefs, I have also shifted many of my perceptions of the world around me and the people with whom I share it.

One way to learn more about our own beliefs is to be open to the convictions of others. Sometimes when we do this, the other person's beliefs resonate with us and we recognize that they hold truth for us also. At other times when we listen, we realize that the other person's beliefs are not meant for us. Either way, we have gained. We have learned a little more about ourselves through either process.

what I hold to be true

My beliefs are not a static thing. I am constantly trying to expand my understanding of the nature of the Universe and my place in it. I have probably only scratched the surface. I have, however, come to some insights based upon my own spiritual experiences and the studying I have done. I am including here an overview of these insights. I offer them to you for your consideration.

First and most importantly, I have come to deeply believe in the existence of a Higher Power. Whether we call that being God, or Higher Power, or the Creator, or the I Am, makes no difference. Each of these names represents the same concept—the creative force that brought us into being. I have used the first three titles interchangeably throughout the book, since those are the designations I most commonly use.

I perceive God as possessing both male and female qualities. In my personal prayers, I address God as, "Mother/Father God." Throughout this book I have chosen to refer to God in the masculine form simply to eliminate the more cumbersome "He/She" designation.

I believe that, being a creative force, God extended Himself and created all that exists. We are literally made up of God energy. Because of this, human beings are divine; we are children of God. Since I view God as embodying the energy of love, I believe that human beings, at their core, do also—despite actions that often seem to contradict this.

At some point in our evolution we began to see ourselves as being separate from God. (Whether this occurred in a physical sense or only mentally is an area of debate.) However it came about, many human beings now experience a sense of detachment from God. What we are seeking is to once again "rejoin" with the source of our being.

we are spiritual beings

I believe that, at our essence, we are spiritual beings. We are not our bodies; we are much more than that. The bodies that we now inhabit are merely vehicles for our spirits.

In an effort to gain the wisdom we need to rejoin with God, we agree to come to earth to learn the lessons our soul is most in need of. Our purpose on earth, then, is to learn these lessons. We have enrolled in an "earth school," if you will.

I believe that we are given many opportunities to experience life in a physical body. We have many chances to learn our lessons in preparation for being reunited with our Creator. It is through this process of repeatedly being in physical form, or reincarnation, that we accumulate the wisdom we are in search of.

our Higher Self

I believe that each of us has a "Higher Self." The Higher Self is the highest point of our consciousness. It is the sum total of awareness that our soul has gleaned through its experiences in both this and other incarnations. It is the part of us that is consciously aware of God and our relationship with Him.

When we incarnate we are an aspect of that Higher Self, not the totality of it. As human beings, we have much more limited awareness. We become forgetful of many aspects of our true spiritual identity. If we are fortunate, as we attend this earth school we will begin to remember who we *truly* are and what we are doing here.

signing up for the journey

I believe that we undertake this earthly experience with a great deal of forethought. We consciously sign up for the journey. I believe we choose, on a soul level, our parents, our children, and the circumstances we will be born into. We do this so that we will have the opportunity to experience the lessons our soul is most in need of. While some of these people and situations will be pleasant and to our liking, others will not. Adversity is sometimes our most powerful teacher.

It is my experience, as I attempt to work on a particular lesson, that one or more situations dealing with that lesson will probably arise. If I am working on communication, for instance, I may find myself being faced with an upsetting conversation with a loved one. The situation challenges me to put into use the lesson I am endeavoring to learn. I have come to view these experiences as "workbook pages." Much like the workbook pages I labored over as a young child in school, they provide me with the opportunity to put into practice what I have just learned.

"Workbook pages" help to anchor the lessons we are learning. When I am in the midst of this process, it is sometimes overwhelming to me. At those times I try to remind myself that *I* am the author of this curriculum and that it has great purpose. I am not a victim of circumstances. On a soul level, I purposefully signed up for these exact experiences so that I could learn.

As we journey through our lives, we have the free will to decide whether or not we will learn the lessons we came here for. In other words, we can procrastinate. We can choose not to grow. By doing so, however, we merely delay the process.

Our fear of growing can both necessitate additional lifetimes and limit our capacity to find true happiness in our current life. Sooner or later, however, I believe we will all make the decision to grow. Once we have accomplished the lessons we need to learn, we will then go back to our true home with God, thereby ending our cycle of incarnations.

a great deal of support

When we incarnate, I believe we do so with a great deal of support from the spirit realm. I believe each of us is assigned a guardian angel (a protective presence who stays with us our entire lifetime), spirit guides (one or a number of friends in spirit who collect around us to provide encouragement and assistance), and other beings who desire to assist in our growth. We did not sign up for our earthly journey unprepared!

Throughout this book I frequently use the term "Spirit." I use this title to mean all nonmaterial beings. I have, in my life, often been given guidance by celestial energies that I know to be positive and helpful. I cannot, however, always tell if it is God, my Higher Self, a guide, or an angel providing me with the assistance. Because of this, I use the generalized term "Spirit" to designate these energies. Even though it is being stated in a singular form, it can refer to one or more beings.

"when I arrive"

I have spent many years consciously learning about both life and myself. This has not been a quick process for me. Initially, when I set upon the path, I thought in terms of "when I arrive." I now doubt that we ever do completely "arrive." As long as we are alive we will continue to be faced with new challenges. We will be given opportunities to replace our old, self-defeating patterns so that we might begin to experience our lives with more ease and less distress.

I have found that, for me, the best way to live my life more consciously is by joining in the process with others. In this way, I am able to benefit from what others have learned, and share with them what I have learned. I deeply believe that this is the way the process of healing works at its best: we support the growth of others and, in doing so, are helped ourselves.

It is with this intention that I have included, in Part 2 of this book, the most important lessons that I have learned on my own healing journey. I offer what has been deeply meaningful to me in hopes that it may be of benefit to you also. I have included, in Part 3, an explanation of the healing activities that have made such a difference in my life.

I invite you to explore these attitudes and activities. I hope that in doing so, you will join me in developing an awareness that we are *all* valuable—even without our cheesecake recipes!

part 2

lessons I have learned

A woman is dying of AIDS. A priest is summoned. He attempts to comfort her, but to no avail.

"I am lost," she said. "I have ruined my life and every life around me. Now I'm going painfully to hell. There is no hope for me."

The priest saw a framed picture of a pretty girl on the dresser. "Who is this?" he asked. The woman brightened. "She is my daughter; the one beautiful thing in my life."

"And would you help her if she was in trouble, or made a mistake? Would you forgive her? Would you still love her?"

"Of course I would!" cried the woman, "I would do anything for her! Why do you ask such a question?"

"Because I want you to know," said the priest, "that God has a picture of *you* on *His* dresser."

Ed McManus quoting a priest's sermon he heard while in Puerto Rico

lesson 1

we must be open to change

...and then the day came when the risk to remain tight in a bud was more painful than the risk it took to blossom.

Anaïs Nin

In order for me to take steps toward healing, I found I needed to be open to new attitudes and beliefs. This was extremely challenging for me as it is, I believe, for most people. It feels so much safer to continue believing that which we have believed our entire lives: attitudes about ourselves, about relationships, about God, about the world.

In hindsight, I now realize that the saying "When the student is ready, the teacher appears" really *is* accurate. In my early 20s I prayed daily to God to heal me and take away my emotional pain. What I was hoping for was a miracle. What I got was just that.

It came in a different form than I was anticipating, though. It came in the form of mentors, friends, long talks, books, counseling, writing, and quotations. It didn't come overnight—although I would have loved it to! Instead, it came bit by bit over time.

My choice to change and grow came from an instinct of self-preservation. I was miserable and didn't want to spend my life feeling depressed, powerless, and of little value.

I have often thought how different my life would have turned out had my mother and brother not died when I was young. Those experiences stirred up questions that I have spent many years trying to answer: "Why are we alive? What *is* the purpose? Is there life after death?"

The deaths of my mother and brother, whom I loved so much, sent me into a spiritual tailspin. I asked myself, "How could God have allowed this to happen? Is there a God at all?" It had been easy for me to believe in Heaven and an afterlife when death was at a safe distance. Now that it was *my* mother and *my* brother, I cared much more deeply. The thought that they might truly be gone—not existing in any form anymore—was the most painful thing I could imagine. I needed to explore the bigger picture of reality and how we all fit into it.

processing new information

I have spent a great number of years searching for answers regarding the nature of our existence. Along the way I learned a helpful method for dealing with all the new information I was trying to process.

When I am exposed to a new idea or belief and it feels accurate to me right away, I incorporate it into my belief system. (There are times when I hear something and the idea immediately resonates with me; I know in my heart it is right for me.) At other times, when I read or hear something that I know is not right for me, I just release it.

But many times I'm not sure. The idea or belief may be something I have never previously considered, and I don't know if it is accurate for me or not. I have learned to reserve judgment at those times. I conjure up an image in my mind of a stove and put the concepts I am undecided about on the back burners. It is a method for storing the new concept until I have sufficient information or experience to either accept it or release it.

I tend to be very discerning (and maybe even skeptical), so the majority of things I hear or read end up on the back burner. Over the years I have come to realize that new ideas are oftentimes like new pieces of furniture. Once a newly purchased coffee table or chair is in my home, it often takes me a period of time to decide if it is a good fit. It is the same with new ideas.

being open to new ideas

I have learned a great deal about myself in the last 25 years. I now know that I am a seeker of truth, and that necessitates my willingness to be open to new ideas even if they seem foreign at first. It means that I have to hold the pursuit of truth higher than my attachment to a particular belief. I am constantly looking for more awareness, more insight, more clarity.

I have come to the realization that developing my spirituality is vitally important because it creates the framework for the way I view myself, the world, and my relationships with others. It is my life's greatest, and most meaningful, challenge.

lesson 2

we need to decide what kind of God we believe in

When we believe that God is Father, we also believe that such a father's hand will never cause his child a needless tear. We may not understand life any better, but we will not resent life any longer.

William Barclay

Metaphysician Carla Neff Gordan tells of going to church as a child. She lived in the South and attended a fundamentalist church. When she was very young she would attend bible school downstairs in the basement while church services went on upstairs. In bible school she was taught that God was a loving father and that she was incredibly precious in His eyes.

As Carla got older, she started attending church services upstairs with the other children her age. Here she heard that God was strict and punished you if you stepped out of line. She says she decided then and there that she wanted to believe in the basement God.

I don't believe it can be both ways. Either God is unconditionally loving and accepting, or God is judgmental and critical. We have to decide how we are going to view our God, because that will greatly impact the relationship we have with Him.

I have come to the conclusion in my own life that God is the basement God. It just doesn't make sense to me otherwise. I relate to God as my parent, and there is absolutely no way that I, as a parent, would look at my daughter or son and condemn them to suffering for all eternity for a mistake they had made, no matter how large the mistake was. I just have to believe that God has an infinitely larger capacity to love unconditionally than I do!

It seems much more logical to me that we are given many chances, over many lifetimes, to do it right. Sometimes it just takes time. Sometimes the way that we learn to do things right is to do them wrong initially. As a child, I stole things on several occasions (candy and a religious item, no less). Looking back at it now, these were invaluable learning experiences for me. Each time after I stole an item, I had an attack of conscience so severe that I developed a stomachache.

From those experiences, I came to the realization that stealing wasn't worth it. I didn't like the way it made me feel. I learned a very important lesson from those childhood transgressions.

It makes sense to me, then, that if I can see the value of learning from mistakes, surely God can also. We just need time to get it right.

what role does God play in your life?

God used to occupy an hour of my thoughts and time on Sunday morning. Now I find a flow of spiritual thoughts woven throughout my day. In fact, the more spiritually-oriented I become, the more I realize there is no difference between spirituality and the everyday activities I am involved in. The everyday activities *are* deeply spiritual.

The way a person lives their daily life reflects their true belief system and values. I used to run to God only when my life was in trouble. Now I start out each day with a few moments of quiet prayer turning my day over to God; asking that I be used as an instrument of light, love, healing, empowerment, and peace. I carry this thought with me throughout my day.

I also start my day by asking for God's help with whatever I will be undertaking that day—conversations, work, challenges. My motivation for actions is no longer based on trying to avoid the judgment of God. I do the things I do now out of a deep desire to work *with* God. I believe this intention to be the surest path to peace of mind and wholeness.

a very important issue to consider

I think it behooves each of us to spend some time grappling with the issue of just who our God/Higher Power is. It is a very important factor in determining our relationship with God and deciding whether we will view the relationship as loving or adversarial.

It is also a very important factor in determining how we will view ourselves and our value (or lack of it). I didn't really appreciate myself until I began to understand that I am part of a benevolent God, and because of that, there is divine purpose to my life and the life of each person.

lesson 3

we are not victims

There is nothing punishing us. There are only revelations to be had. We are only put in situations to expand.

Karen Boland

One of the biggest shifts I needed to make on my road to wholeness was in my attitude about being a victim. I grew up feeling as though I didn't have much control in my life. That feeling was heightened incredibly with the loss of my mother and brother. It felt as though the rug had been pulled out from under me and there was nothing I could do about it. I felt like a puppet. Someone (or something) else was in control of my life.

I even approached parenthood this way. It was "what women did" in the 1970s when they were married. I don't really remember ever making a conscious choice, or even realizing that I had the right to make a choice, about whether or not to have children.

I look at my life so differently now, these many years later. It has become so very important to me to live my life as consciously as possible. I understand now that I am not a victim.

After years of metaphysical study, and a great deal of soul searching, I have come to the conclusion that life isn't something that happens *to* us. Rather, it is a process that we agree to participate in for the purpose of furthering our soul's growth (and ultimately reuniting with God).

When we incarnate we become forgetful (to a greater or lesser degree, depending upon the individual) about the nature of this true reality. We forget that we chose to come to earth. We forget that, on a soul level, we chose our parents, our children, and our circumstances because they would offer us opportunities for growth. We forget why we are really here and that we have spiritual assistance if we but ask.

how do you view yourself?

I view my life very differently when I come from the perspective that I am not a human being having a spiritual experience, but rather, a spiritual being having a human experience. I think we are literally part of God—made from God energy—and that what we are undertaking is a divine experience.

When we view ourselves as victims, we shortchange ourselves in so many ways. We channel our energy into thoughts of "poor me." We tend to isolate ourselves emotionally and, at times, physically. We delude ourselves into thinking that we are alone...abandoned by God.

Nothing could be further from the truth. Spiritual assistance is a given. It is our birthright. Our challenge is to learn to ask for it and be open to it. Humans have free will, and we can either choose to invite the gift of guidance into our lives, or we can choose to live without it.

I believe there are *many* loving beings in spirit who wish to help us. (Perhaps it is a sense of unworthiness that prevents us from accepting this fact.) I often wonder if they don't look lovingly at us as we flounder and think, "I would love to help you, but because I need to honor your free will, I am limited until you ask for assistance."

The more open and receptive I become, the more joyful my life gets. That certainly doesn't mean that I don't face my share of problems; it just means I realize now that there is purpose in what I am doing and that I don't have to go it alone.

we can choose our response

It is obvious to all of us who have been emotionally knocked to our knees that we do not have complete control over our life. I do not mean to imply that we do. What we do have control over, however, is our *response* to life.

Look around you. Perhaps you know people who have gone through adversity—a divorce, job loss, childhood abuse, the death of a loved one—and come out the other end stronger and wiser. It is in our capacity for growth that we can make a conscious choice to heal. We can *choose* to bring forth good out of what was so painful to us. When we view ourselves as victims we prevent ourselves from taking these healing steps; we handicap ourselves.

When my mother died, I couldn't conceive of any possible good coming from the experience. I still miss her deeply—I know I always will. Mother's Day will probably always stir up a sense of loss in me as it has these 30 years since she passed away.

I am aware now, however, that even painful experiences offer us gifts if we are willing to be open to them. Experiencing my mother's and my brother's deaths taught me a great deal about compassion. I believe I am a much more sensitive person than I would have been otherwise. I am not afraid to be with those who are experiencing the pain of having lost a loved one. I know that there are no magical words to heal their wounds, but I also know that just being there and loving them can be of great assistance.

It is truly amazing to me how, time and again, Spirit has brought into my life women who have recently lost their mothers and are in deep pain. It is such an honor for me to be able to hug them, love them, and listen quietly to them. They know that I understand their pain and it is healing for both of us.

saying "thank you"

I once heard Oprah Winfrey talk about the profound impact her mentor, Maya Angelou, has had on her life. She said that when she calls Maya and is upset about an issue, Maya calms her down by reminding her first to say "thank you" for the situation; "thank you" for the opportunity for growth that the situation contains.

I decided to experiment with saying "thank you" to Spirit when I was faced with difficult circumstances. I found that there was, in fact, great value to doing this.

I have found that when I say "thank you," it seems to change the energy of the situation. It becomes more positive. I begin to remember that I am not a victim and that my life is part of a divine plan. I also begin to remember that what looks like a negative thing today might be the exact experience necessary to teach me what I need to learn.

an opportunity to choose

Several years ago I was faced with a situation that was very challenging for me. After working seven and a half years at a small firm, I was told I was being laid off. I was being replaced by my employer's wife.

I knew it had been a very difficult year economically, so the lay-off wasn't totally unexpected. When my employer gently broke the news to me, I realized that I could choose to react in several different ways: I could get angry; I could be resentful; or, I could remember that I am not a victim and look at this as an opportunity for growth. I chose the latter.

I decided I would trust that my soul knew where I needed to be. I don't mean to whitewash the situation. It was very difficult emotionally. I loved the people I worked with and felt heartsick at leaving them. It was upsetting to me to leave the security of a long-term job. But I worked very hard to keep as my focus the awareness that I was *not* a victim and that this change that looked to be negative was really very positive and necessary for my growth. I worked at saying "thank you" to Spirit.

It has been several years since that experience and I see clearly now that it was a necessary step for me to take. I needed to be on my way in my life's work. Had I not been laid off, I wouldn't have experienced the job that followed it, which taught me a great deal about myself. It taught me that I was far more capable than I had ever thought.

I understand now that being laid off was in the master plan for my life. The experience was a "workbook" page in realizing that we are not victims. It taught me a great deal about how we can make a conscious choice to react to the circumstances in our life.

understanding the big picture

Standing back and viewing our life in a larger perspective can be very helpful when we deal with problems and challenges. That doesn't mean that we won't experience emotional turmoil when difficulties arise. We are human and experience the world with great emotion at times. Often, I need to express my feelings about a situation—the frustration, the sadness, the anger—before I can get myself calmer and more centered. It is very grounding to then take a step back and try to understand the larger picture.

I do this by asking myself questions that are so vitally important: "What can I learn from this situation? What is my Higher Self trying to teach me?" When we can remember that we are spiritual students, we are empowered. These questions are a reminder that we are not victims; that there is great purpose in what we are going through. By looking at experiences as lessons we are more able to gracefully weather the situation and see the value in it.

Not long ago I saw a talk show on which two Vietnam veterans spoke about the years they spent as prisoners of war. They talked about being tortured and living in isolation for many years. The talk show host asked them how it was that they had such positive outlooks on the world now, why they weren't bitter or cynical. They replied that the turning point for both of them came when they stopped asking "Why me, God?" and changed it to "Show me, God."

Instead of being a victim, they searched for the meaning. They looked for the purpose of their adversity. They came to the conclusion that all people are isolated and live in self-imposed prisons at times—attitudes that hold them down. These two men now travel across the country speaking about how people can grow from difficult experiences.

It is challenging to stand back and look at our lives from a larger perspective. Oftentimes our initial reaction will be to think, "Poor me!" when faced with an upsetting experience. I find that the longer I pursue the path of personal growth, the shorter the "poor me" phase lasts because I am uncomfortable with the powerlessness that attitude brings. The sooner I can regain my grounding and perspective, the sooner I can ask for clarity and begin to deal with the situation.

When I ask myself, "What can I learn from this situation? What is my Higher Self trying to teach me?" I can then begin to understand what it is my soul is in such need of knowing and remembering. It is then that I can regain my strength and begin to work on the lessons at hand.

lesson 4

we are not on this path alone

For every soul, there is a guardian watching over it.

The Koran

I do not think we would choose to incarnate if we didn't have the resources to back us up. After all, while Earth is an incredibly beautiful place and life holds the potential for much happiness, life also holds the potential for deep emotional and physical pain. I truly don't think we are expected to go it alone.

We live in an age where science is worshipped and there is a great deal of skepticism surrounding anything that cannot be proven scientifically. It took me many years to come to the conclusion that there is much that cannot be readily known by our five senses. We enrich our world immeasurably when we trust ourselves to go beyond our physical limitations and into our "inner knowingness."

When we open ourselves to realms beyond that which we can taste, touch, see, hear, and smell, we expand our perspective of both reality and ourselves. We can then, with our free will, consciously begin to invite spiritual assistance into our lives.

taking the first step

I was skeptical for many years about the role of Spirit in my life. I had become estranged from God. I blamed Him for the painful experiences in my life. I wasn't convinced that He was benevolent and I didn't know if I could trust this distant being.

My spiritual awareness has grown from the bottom up. It seems to me that most people would begin with a relationship with God, and learning how to trust from that experience, would then expand it outward to their Higher Self, their spirit guides, the angels, etc. I needed to do it the other way around. I needed to start with spiritual beings that felt less threatening to me—the angels.

Having grown up Catholic, I was comfortable with the concept of angels. I had always thought of them as benevolent and caring, so I decided to try working with them. I wanted to see if angels really existed and, if they did, if I could establish a relationship with them.

developing a relationship with angels

I decided to start in a very down-to-earth, practical way. I began to experiment at our large, local supermarket.

I began by making a request of the angels as I would approach the store to do my weekly grocery shopping. I would respectfully explain that I wanted to work with them, if possible. On several occasions I was feeling lonely and asked if they would bring me into contact with someone I knew and with whom I could share a hug. On other occasions, when I was feeling "filled up," I would offer to have a conversation with someone who was in need of companionship.

After I made the request, I would let it go and not dwell on it. I would put it out of my mind and go about the task of grocery shopping. Oftentimes it wasn't until I was in my car on the way home that I would remember the request I had made of the angels. It was then that I would start to realize I *had* seen a former neighbor and was given a hug, or that a stranger had started a conversation with me in the produce section.

At first, I was very skeptical. I chalked a number of experiences up to coincidence. Slowly, however, as more and more experiences accumulated, I realized that they could no longer be explained away as coincidence. I began to recognize that I *was* developing a relationship with the angels.

I found that the most effective way of working with them was to make my request (or an offer to help), and then put it out of my mind. If, on the way home, I realized that nothing had happened that day, I tried to remain open-minded. Perhaps there was a reason of which I was just not aware.

Learning to work with the angels was not a quick process. I was very skeptical initially so it took quite a long time—and a lot of experimenting—for me to recognize that angels did exist and that they were willing to work with me. As time went on I began to recognize more and more instances of their responding to my request. I began to see situations in which they were working through me to touch other people.

learning to trust

I think that I needed to start with the angels because I felt so alienated from God for so long; I felt so angry. I didn't know if I was dealing with a basement God or an upstairs God. I didn't know if I was dealing with a benevolent entity or one that was waiting to judge my every action. This uncertainty made it very difficult for me to trust in God.

I needed to take small steps toward developing a relationship with Spirit; I needed to feel safe in the process. Experimenting by working with the angels was something I could do without a great deal of fear. It allowed me to venture out safely into the area of working with Spirit.

Looking back, I wonder if one of the reasons I struggled so with the idea of spiritual assistance is that I didn't truly think I was worthy of Spirit's involvement in my life. I had a type of "me and them" attitude— I thought that Spirit and I were in two separate realities and weren't particularly connected.

I no longer view our relationship in that way. It is much closer and more personal now. I have come to the realization that Spirit cares deeply about my life and how I am doing. I regularly seek guidance from God, Spirit guides, my Higher Self and the angels—including my own guardian angel.

opening to the process

I have found that the more I open my awareness to Spirit, the easier it is for these beings to work with me. I have begun to trust the process of working with them. I now know that they don't mind my asking for assistance in everyday matters. In fact, I think they are delighted at being asked.

I respectfully enlist Spirit's help in a multitude of ways, asking for assistance in everything from discovering my life's purpose to decorating my home. I ask for guidance when relationship challenges surface, for the protection and safekeeping of my loved ones, and for assistance in making decisions on items I am going to purchase. I have come to realize that they are willing to help with every aspect of my life.

It is my understanding that Spirit cannot go against our free will. I suspect these beings wait patiently by, doing what they can, until they are invited to participate more actively in our lives. It is with our free will that we choose the degree to which we will be receptive to working with spiritual beings.

One very important lesson I have learned about working with Spirit, though, is that their time frame is not always the same as mine. I need to use patience. I make a request, thank them in advance for their guidance and help, and take whatever actions I need to take in the meantime.

I have also found that saying "thank you" to them when I make the request is much more effective than begging. When I thank them I am trusting that they will, in fact, help and I remain more receptive to them.

When I "beg" it seems to set up an almost unconscious feeling that I am not really going to receive what I am asking for. Thanking the angels seems to make it easier for them to work with me.

I wonder if many people work with Spirit without even consciously knowing it. It lies in the quick, "Please help me find a parking space" or "Please help me find my purse." As our awareness of Spirit's assistance in our life expands, we realize that it isn't a coincidence when someone pulls out of a parking space just as we approach or that our lost purse is returned intact.

At first it is easy for us to think, "Well, that was just a coincidence." As we become more and more aware of working with Spirit, though, we realize that there are just too many of these experiences to dismiss them…too many times when, whether or not anyone else knows it, *we* know we have been helped; too many times when we know in our hearts that they have worked through us to reach other people.

Working with Spirit is now one of my life's greatest joys. I hold the experiences close to my heart, and I am deeply grateful for them.

receiving spiritual guidance and assistance

During the past year I have had a number of conversations with a dear friend who is trying to understand how a person receives spiritual guidance. In the past she had always interpreted guidance to mean that a person would literally hear God talking to them. While I'm sure that's an experience some people have, that's not the way I experience it. For me it is much subtler, much less obvious. It is not so much a shout as it is a whisper.

I can identify with my friend's confusion about spiritual guidance. I have come to recognize it as something quite different than what I was initially expecting. I previously thought that guidance would feel as though it came from "outside of myself"—as though someone else was talking to me. Instead, I most commonly experience it as coming from within myself.

Oftentimes, for me, it comes in the form of a "knowingness." It feels like I am being guided to speak to a particular person, or attend a certain event, or take a particular course of action. I do not experience this as a voice; it is more like an intuitive feeling. I just know it feels like the right thing to do.

I have also come to recognize that I often receive guidance when I am least expecting it. A "thought" will pop into my mind when I am doing a mundane activity such as driving, or showering, or taking a walk. Oftentimes the thought will be an insight into something I am working on; a fresh perspective, something that hadn't occurred to me before. I used to dismiss these thoughts as just being my own; as originating from within myself. I am coming to realize that they are, instead, forms of spiritual assistance.

Guidance can come to us in many other ways as well. Spirit uses many forms to communicate with us—meditation, books, music, other people, animals, channeled readings, nature, synchronicities, etc. In fact, there are probably as many different ways for Spirit to communicate with people as there are people. If we sincerely request their guidance we will be shown the methods that are effective for us.

I have found that some of the best ways for me to receive guidance are through meditation, journaling, automatic writing, and being out in nature. (Automatic writing is writing that is done when you are in a very relaxed and receptive state of mind. I explain this process further in Part 3 on Healing Activities.) The most important thing we can do to receive guidance is to *ask for it* and trust that it will be given.

Spiritual guidance is always positive and loving in its nature. It is always for the highest good of all. We do not, in any way, give up our free will when we listen to Spirit. We always retain the right to choose what we will do with the information we receive. I have found that my life is enriched a great deal, however, when I *do* listen and follow their promptings. I have often been amazed at the wonderful results that come from being open to their wisdom and guidance.

As we gain a deeper understanding of Spirit's love for us, it becomes easier to be open to the various manners in which they assist us. For example, several years ago my daughter had a beautiful gray and white rabbit named Binny. We kept Binny in the house and he was a wonderful pet.

I became very attached to Binny and knew in my heart that there was something very spiritual about this rabbit. If I was upset or out-of-sorts, all I had to do was spend a few minutes petting him before I would feel a sense of peace come over me. When he passed away I was deeply saddened. I truly believe that Spirit was able to work through Binny to bring me peace and comfort. He was a spiritual gift to me and I am very grateful for his presence in my life.

becoming part of the process

I have found a progression in my experience of working with Spirit. I very much identify with the words of Hudson Taylor, "I used to ask God to help me. Then I asked if I might help Him. I ended up by asking God to do His work through me."

Once I realized that Spirit was actually willing to work with me, I found the prospect very exciting. I was very grateful for receiving divine assistance in my life, and I wanted to be a channel of that assistance for others. In everyday activities I now consciously open myself to being a conduit for Spirit's words and love.

For me, there is nothing quite like those moments when I am consciously aware that I am working in partnership with Spirit. I never lose the fresh sense of awe that accompanies the experience. It is a heart-expanding feeling; a feeling of being on course in my life. Working with Spirit stirs up a deep sense of honor in me. I feel humbled at the privilege. I never get over my amazement at the workings of Spirit and how deeply we are loved and valued.

lesson 5

we must learn to love ourselves

The remarkable thing is that we really love our neighbor as ourselves; we do unto others as we do unto ourselves. We hate others when we hate ourselves. We are tolerant toward others when we tolerate ourselves. We forgive others when we forgive ourselves. It is not love of self but hatred of self which is at the root of troubles that afflict our world.

Eric Hoffer

It becomes increasingly clear to me, the older I get, that the most important thing I can do in this lifetime is to learn to truly love myself. This is no easy task for someone who was raised to believe that it is sinful to think too much of yourself. (Pride—one of the Seven Deadly Sins!)

I used to believe that thinking too highly of yourself would lead to vanity, a lack of humility, and moral decay. I have found loving and accepting myself to bring about just the opposite. The more I nurture and truly love myself, the more I am able to love others.

Loving myself unconditionally is a major challenge. It is a long road and I have a great distance yet to go. I have made significant progress, though, and I am most appreciative for the growth.

I am deeply grateful to friends, family members, mentors, and spiritual guides who have loved me even when I thought I was at my most unlovable—who somehow saw value and goodness in me even when I couldn't see it for myself. Step by step they help to heal the parts of me that lie so deep within, the parts that surge forth with shame and insecurity when I least expect it.

self-talk

When I was in counseling years ago, I made the comment to my therapist that I was much kinder to other people than I was to myself. She commented, "I think you aren't being honest with yourself. If you are being judgmental and critical with yourself, you *are* doing it to others also." I chafed at her saying that and decided I would observe my own thoughts and prove her wrong.

Unfortunately, I found that she wasn't wrong. What I observed was that I was, in fact, very judgmental of others, just as I was of myself. I started seeing a correlation between my thoughts about myself and my thoughts about others. It was humbling for me to realize, for example, that my intolerance toward my own eating habits likewise caused me to be critical of the eating habits of others.

I began to observe that the way we talk to *ourselves* is evident in the way we speak to others. Several years ago I attended a memorial service for the father of a very dear friend. A relative of hers, an elderly woman, approached my friend and said very forcefully, "Buck up—we've all been through this!"

My first reaction was to be appalled. (I had never heard anything so callous said to a person in mourning.) My second reaction was one of empathy and pity. I thought how very painful it must be to be that woman. Her saying that to someone else, at a time of such vulnerability, was a reflection of her inner dialogues with herself. On another occasion, when she was experiencing the pain of losing someone, did she say sternly to herself, "Buck up!"? How many times had she denied herself the healing benefits of honoring her own feelings?

This issue of self-talk is a very important one if we hope to live in peace with ourselves. In 1986 Shad Helmstetter published *What To Say When You Talk To Your Self*. I found the book to be an eye opener. I had never really given much thought, prior to that, about the way I spoke *to* myself.

As I started paying attention, however, I was appalled at the number of critical thoughts that I directed at myself. I found myself thinking, "Well that was a stupid thing to do!" when I accidentally bumped into a table corner, or "How could I be so dumb?" when I made a mistake.

It occurred to me that, at times, I was my own worst enemy. As I monitored my self-talk I realized that I would never choose to be around someone who was so judgmental and critical, and yet, this was how I harangued myself day after day.

As I have started to gain a larger perspective of my life and myself as a spiritual being, it has become easier to treat myself with respect. I have learned a new way of speaking to myself; of talking to myself as I would a beloved friend. I have found this to be an important aspect of treating myself more gently.

When I am upset I try to remember to speak kindly to myself. "Take a deep breath, sweetheart. You are safe. I will help you." Think of how you would speak to an agitated child. It is important that we learn to treat ourselves with that same degree of compassion and love.

replenishing ourselves

In my early years of parenting I didn't know that I needed to nurture myself. I thought being a good parent meant devoting *all* of your time to your children, meeting their needs without a thought of your own. I realize now that in doing so, I really shortchanged them—especially my daughter. As a young child, she had a mother who was often depressed and frustrated. I would give anything now to be able to go back and change that.

A turning point for me was reading a quote by Mother Teresa: "To keep a lamp burning, we have to keep putting oil in it." When I read that quote I realized that I had expected myself to be a well that could always be drawn upon without being filled back up. It was an awakening to me to come to the conclusion that instead, I was like a lamp and *did* need consistent replenishing.

My life has a great deal more balance now and, consequently, I have more to offer my children. The replenishing has taken many forms over the years: going to therapy to learn healthier attitudes and beliefs; taking classes to nurture my mind; going to spiritual retreats to nurture my soul; spending time with loving, supportive friends and family members; writing; taking long walks; spending time by myself.

Over the years I have become more adept at realizing when the oil in my lamp is running low. I am more sensitive to my own needs now, so I am not as likely to burn myself out.

One of the advantages of getting older is that I have had more time to get to know myself. It is much easier for me now to think, "If I do this thing which is draining, I am going to need some replenishing time afterwards." I schedule that into my week. It is important that we value ourselves enough to take good care of ourselves. If we don't, everyone loses in the long run.

appreciating our gifts

I have come to realize that one aspect of loving ourselves involves developing an honest appreciation for our strengths and our talents. In my quest to be humble I often dismissed people's compliments. I now realize that those compliments were gifts that had the potential to help teach me about myself.

I have learned that it doesn't serve me well to downplay my strengths. When I don't honor them and recognize them as valuable, I am less likely to develop my strengths and share them.

Several years ago Tom and I went out to dinner with a man we both admired. He was a teacher and a professional speaker and one of his outstanding qualities was a gorgeous voice—deep and warm. I told him how very much I liked his voice. He surprised me by answering, "Thank you. It was a gift I was blessed with and I'm very grateful for it."

I have thought of his words many times throughout the years and have decided that if I were God and had given someone that wonderful voice, I would want them to respect and appreciate it like this man did. I would not want them to respond to a compliment with, "You know, it's really not all that special" or an insincere "Really? I never noticed."

The more I start to recognize the gifts that I was born with, the more I take responsibility for using them to make a difference in the world. The more I come to view myself as someone who has something valuable to share, the more courage I have to share it.

If you are not sure what your gifts are, you can begin to discover them by listening to what others say when they are complimenting you. I know that it can be embarrassing and awkward to receive compliments, but try to really pay attention to them. If they are sincere, they will tell you a great deal about yourself.

valuing our time

Part of learning to love ourselves means learning to value our time. It means giving ourselves the same respect we would give others. It can take many forms but the message is crucial.

Many years ago I had a friend who was in the habit of calling me late in the evening. I was married and our daughter was an active toddler at the time. Late evening, after she was in bed, was a precious time to me. It was the only time in my day when I was truly "off duty." It was a slice of peace and quiet that I could spend either with my husband or by myself.

Night after night my friend called and proceeded to tell me about her day at great length. The conversation usually lasted over an hour.

As I look back at that experience now, I realize that I placed a much higher value on her needs than mine. Even though I cringed every time the phone rang late in the evening, I never once told her about my needs. I was too afraid to risk her disapproval by telling her I wanted that time to myself.

It was a frustrating and painful experience for me but it ended up teaching me a great deal. I learned the hard way about the price I pay when I am not honest about my own needs. I also began to see that being "nice" (instead of being truthful) in a relationship does far more damage than good. I may have been nice to her, but underneath I was seething with resentment. I am much more truthful with my friends now and, consequently, have much healthier friendships.

self-centered vs. selfish

Webster's Dictionary defines "self-centered" as meaning the same thing as "selfish." I wish I had the power to change that. If I could, I would give the word "self-centered" a new definition. It would read something like this: "self-centered—a positive state of being wherein one is centered within oneself; an appreciation of self that enables a person to likewise see the value in others."

I have found that the more I appreciate myself and recognize that I am a unique human being with strengths and talents, the more I am able to make a difference in the world. When I am centered and feeling good about myself, I am able to reach out easily to others. When I am "off-center" and critical of myself, I feel much more inhibited about sharing myself for fear people will disapprove of me in the same way I disapprove of myself.

I was raised Roman Catholic in the 1950s and was taught (as were people of many different religions) that being selfish is a serious sin. As a result, I grew up always placing others' needs above my own. Whenever I heard God's commandment "Love your neighbor *as yourself*" I somehow forgot about the second half of it.

It never occurred to me that I was supposed to treat myself as respectfully as I treated others. That does *not* mean that I don't take the needs of others into consideration. What it means is that I honor my own needs in addition to the other person's, so that we *both* might benefit.

I have found that honoring myself has caused me to be much more honest in my relationships. In the past I would say "yes" to another person's request or invitation whether or not I really wanted to perform the service or attend the function. Now, I pause a moment and get in touch with my inner self. I ask myself whether I can fulfill their request with a clear, loving heart or if it would make me feel resentful. If it is the latter, I tactfully decline.

I found initially that family and friends would take offense at times when I honored my own needs. They weren't accustomed to it. They were still operating under our old pattern of "saying yes whether or not we wanted to" and then resenting the other person afterward. In the long run I have found that respecting my time and energy has improved my relationships with others. I know it has certainly improved my relationship with myself!

gentleness toward others

I have come to the realization that my attitudes about myself directly influence my attitudes about others. As I have become gentler with myself, I find I have also become gentler with others. I have learned that we are not different from other human beings; we are the same. We are all souls who have incarnated with the hope of advancing in our learning process.

I believe each of us is doing the best we know how to do at any given moment. As Maya Angelou says, "If we knew better we'd have done better." I have yet to run across anyone who purposefully set out to make a mess of their life. We are all students trying to learn our lessons the best way we know how.

When we treat others with harshness, instead of gentleness, it has repercussions in our own lives. When we shout at the driver who just cut us off, "What an idiot! How could you be so stupid?" we are giving ourselves the message that people *can* be stupid. I do not for a moment believe that. I think we are divine reflections of God. If you drive an automobile and are truthful with yourself, can you really say you have *never* made a mistake? Does it mean then that *you* are stupid?

In judging others so harshly we paint ourselves with the same brush. It subtly affects the way we view ourselves. People can, and do, act in ways that are careless, aggressive, and at times even dangerous, but I believe that human beings, because of their innate divinity, are not stupid.

When we set ourselves in judgment of others, we are attempting to do something that we really aren't qualified to do. We don't have all the facts. We aren't privy to the larger perspective of a situation and its participants. We do not know the history of a person (both in this lifetime and in previous lives) that may have motivated their actions.

I would suspect that frequently people don't even know why they act as they do. I am a very introspective person and, even then, I know I certainly couldn't explain all of my actions, feelings, and fears. Perhaps it behooves us to take a gentler approach to others—to step down from the role of judge. (Why did we think we belonged there in the first place?)

Perhaps our time would be better spent turning our eyes on ourselves, looking at areas where *we* could improve. It's tough being human. It can be scary, confusing, overwhelming, and frustrating. We don't need others judging us. We need their compassion. We are living our lives the best way we know how. So are our neighbors.

lesson 6

honesty really is the best policy

The shortest and surest way to live with honor in the world is to be in reality what we appear to be.

Socrates

In traveling my path of healing I have developed a great deal of respect for honesty. I have come to see it as the foundation I want for relationships with both others and myself. I think many of us are terrified to show others who we really are for fear of rejection. To reveal ourselves openly and honestly takes the rawest kind of courage. If *we* aren't sure that we are lovable, how can we trust that others will find us acceptable?

In my late 20s I had the good fortune to become friends with Tena, a woman who deeply valued honesty and practiced it in her relationships. It was a significantly different way of relating to the world than the way in which I was accustomed.

I learned a great deal from her. I learned that my pattern of always being "nice" had prevented me from being truthful about my feelings. I learned that I could express my wishes and desires without hurting others, and that it could be done with love. As our friendship deepened, I felt safe to begin talking about those parts of myself that I had kept hidden: my anger; my resentments; my feelings of worthlessness.

I realize now, these many years later, what a wonderful gift Tena gave me. When I came to the awareness that she could accept me despite my shortcomings, I became much braver about reaching out to others. As I expanded into more honest relationships with family and friends, I found that the conversations likewise gave them permission to be more truthful with me. What I discovered was that each of us has areas we want to hide—parts of ourselves we are convinced are unlovable—and that it is incredibly healing to bring these areas of ourselves into the light.

learning to listen to ourselves

There are many different aspects to living your life more honestly. The first step I took was to pay attention to the way I really felt about things. I had spent so many years trying to be agreeable (so people would like me) that I had lost touch with what I truly wanted. If a friend asked my preference of a restaurant for lunch, I would invariably say, "It doesn't matter. Where would *you* like to go?" If someone asked me to do him or her a favor that I didn't want to do, I would do it anyway rather than risk his or her disapproval.

I do not know if I was in touch with my inner desires at a young age and then stopped listening to them, or if I never was in touch with them to begin with. All I know is that I became a young woman without a voice; someone who felt that it was much too risky to be truthful about what she wanted.

Changing that pattern was not an easy task for me. I became motivated to change, however, when I started seeing the results of not being truthful. I found that when I did things I did not want to do, I ended up secretly resenting the other person *and* becoming angry with myself. The suppressed anger and resentment damaged *both* my relationship with the other person and with myself.

I consciously decided that this was not how I wanted to live my life, so I set out to change it. Bit by bit, incident by incident, I tried to be more honest in saying how I truly felt about things.

One of the things I have learned along the way is that I have to allow myself time to think about what I want. I don't always immediately know. I am learning to give myself a few moments (or a few hours, or days, depending on how large the issue is), before I make a decision. I have had to *learn* to listen to myself and ask myself what it is that I truly want.

a learning opportunity

As I worked on honestly expressing my preferences, a number of experiences occurred that put the lesson I was learning to the test. Because of my pattern of being unassertive, the experiences were very upsetting to me.

One of these situations involved drapes I had asked a seamstress to make for our new home. I had ordered custom-made draperies for our living room and dining room, both of which had several windows. When the drapes arrived, and were put up, I immediately knew that there was a problem. The color of the fabric wasn't right.

It took an entire weekend, and a lot of tears, before I generated the courage to make a phone call to the seamstress to address the problem. I felt like a "troublemaker" and worried that she would dislike me if I complained. During the course of our conversation she reluctantly told me that the fabric *wasn't* the exact shade I had chosen but she had decided it was "close enough."

It was extremely difficult for me to tell her that I wanted her to remake the drapes, in the correct color, without additional cost to me. She was clearly upset with my request and it turned into a very difficult situation. Ultimately, she did sew new drapes with the correct material at no extra charge.

Today, I am very grateful for that experience with the seamstress. I believe it was a "workbook page" my soul created so that I could learn more about honoring and listening to myself. Because of it, I came to see more clearly the real source of my anxiety: my fear of disapproval—of having someone think I was "not nice." When I chose to make the phone call, and be truthful with the seamstress about my displeasure, I gave myself a powerful message—that my opinion *does* matter. I learned much through that experience.

a deeper level of honesty with ourselves

As I worked on becoming more aware of what I truly wanted, I also felt the need to deepen my honesty with myself. I recognized the importance of acknowledging not only my preferences, but my feelings and attitudes as well. One of the most effective methods that I have used—and still use—to come to a deeper level of honesty within myself is journaling.

I have found my journal to be an invaluable tool in gaining self-awareness because it is such a safe space to explore my thoughts and feelings. It is for my eyes alone. I can express myself anytime, anywhere, without fear of another person's reactions.

When I am filled with emotion, journaling acts as the valve on a pressure cooker. I can rant, I can rave; I can express anger, indignation, or whatever strong feeling I may be experiencing. I can safely express anything I want to. My journal is like the very best of all confidantes. It is always available, always accepting, never judgmental. It has become a friend to me.

Journaling has helped me understand more about the person I really am. Often, it has taken great courage for me to honestly acknowledge my feelings. I have had to come face to face with the fact that I can have deep feelings of anger, resentment, fear, and envy. We all have both the light and the shadow within us. The light is easy to acknowledge, but it takes strength and courage to face the darker aspects of ourselves.

I have discovered that when I give voice to my feelings I take the first step toward understanding their origin in my psyche. Frequently, after I have written about my anger/frustration/confusion, etc., I start getting down to the *real* issue; the *real* reason why I am hurting. I can then use this insight as a step to improve the troubling situation.

Through the process of journaling, I am learning to be more compassionate with myself. I am learning to understand more about myself and, as I do, have come to realize that beneath my strong emotion usually lies a frightened little child.

honesty in relationships

I have found that the more I am truthful with myself, the more I desire to have open, truthful relationships with others. Since I had spent most of my life *not* saying what I *really* thought, being truthful with others was a major challenge. One of my biggest problems was that I didn't know what it meant to be really honest with another person. I was fearful that it meant hurting others.

I have come to learn that being honest with another does *not* mean that we have license to say whatever crosses our mind. ("She asked me if I liked her dress. I thought it was ugly so I told her so.") True honesty is, instead, rooted in compassion and love.

Compassionate truthfulness is a way of building bridges to other people. It is a way of showing others who we really are and what is in our heart. It creates a deeper sense of security in relationships because it enables us to more genuinely know the other person.

I have developed a deep respect for those around me who will lovingly tell me the truth. If I am going clothes shopping, for instance, my very first choice for a companion is my daughter because I know she will be truthful with me and that is what I want. If something I'm trying on doesn't look good, Mandy will tactfully tell me so. ("That dress really doesn't do you justice, Mom. We can do better.")

I know that there are times when the situation is awkward for Mandy; times when it would be much easier for her to say, "It looks fine." Sometimes I have flights of fancy and want to wear a style much better suited to a size six frame than to my still-ample body. Because she knows that what I want is honest feedback, however, she bravely tells me the truth…even if it isn't what I want to hear at the moment. She risks seeing the look of disappointment on my face knowing that, in the end, I will be grateful for her honesty…and I always am.

developing deeper relationships

I am incredibly blessed in my life. I have both friends and family members that I can have deep, open, heart-to-heart conversations with; conversations where we can share what's really going on in our lives. I have worked very hard to help create, and nurture, these relationships.

I didn't always have this in my life. I had to grow into it. When I was younger, my relationships tended to be much more superficial. I was terrified of letting people get too close for fear they would disapprove of me and then leave me.

I felt that there was so very much about myself that was unlovable—my anger, my fears, my depression. (After all, I didn't approve of myself; why ever would someone else?) I thought that if I kept people at a distance, and showed them the face I *thought* they wanted to see, that I would be much safer. What I didn't know at that time, however, was that putting up that wall—that false persona—contributed to my feeling isolated and in pain.

Learning to be more open has been a long, gradual process for me. I discovered along the way that I needed to use a great deal of discretion in deciding how vulnerable I wanted to be in a relationship; that I needed to choose wisely.

I am careful of what I say to people who are critical and highly judgmental, for instance, for I know that they will most likely also treat me with criticism and judgment. I am likewise guarded around people who cannot keep a confidence. I save my innermost thoughts and feelings for friends and family members who will treat them (and me) with respect and compassion. These close, intimate relationships have developed over time.

The process of revealing ourselves, even in emotionally safe environments, can be frightening. Many times I have said to my close friends, "I'm really embarrassed to tell you this about myself..." My fear is that they will leave me if I show them who I really am. What I have found, however, is that they do not leave. Instead, my willingness to be open often gives them permission to share with me their own areas of vulnerability.

In their acceptance of my painful areas, and my acceptance of theirs, we have come to a much deeper understanding of what it means to be human. We have also taken significant strides in healing those issues that once caused us so much discomfort. Like the children's fable *The Velveteen Rabbit*, we have loved each other into being real.

resolving conflict through honesty

As a child, on a number of occasions, I would lie in my bed at night and listen to my father yell at my mother. She would become quiet and not answer back. It was very frightening to me. Because of that, I promised myself I would never have arguments if I ever got married. For a number of years after Tom and I were married, we never argued. We didn't talk about issues that contained conflict. We both believed that it was important to keep the peace at all cost. We were wrong. Just because we weren't dealing with issues **didn't** mean that they went away.

Instead of addressing our feelings, Tom and I held them within, causing a great deal of resentment on both of our parts. Eventually, we came to the realization that this pattern was seriously damaging our relationship. It took a very conscious decision, and a great deal of courage, for us to begin changing these old patterns of relating. We started to understand that we needed to be honest with each other— even if it entailed conflict.

Because of the depth of my childhood aversion to arguments, this has been particularly challenging work for me. Conflict made me feel extremely unsafe. When faced with a serious issue with another person, I would feel a great deal of anxiety—almost panic. It would take me days to build up the courage to have a conversation with the person…to say to them, "I have a problem with what you did."

My greatest teacher in learning how to address conflict has been my son, Matthew. Matt and I are both passionate people at heart and capable of feeling strong emotions. As a young teenager, Matt and I ran into a number of situations where we disagreed—most often having to do with his freedom. We had very different opinions on whether or not he should be able to attend unchaperoned parties, how late he could stay out, whether or not he could go to R-rated movies, etc.

In order to be a responsible parent to Matt, I realized that I had to face my aversion to conflict and be willing to set the limits that I thought were best for him—even if it meant that in the short run he might be incredibly angry with me. He and I had a number of arguments during those years. We both felt strongly about our positions.

What I saw evolving out of these sessions was a very important pattern. After the initial, often emotional encounter, we would both begin to calm down. Slowly we would start to get past the surface issue that we had been disagreeing about and get down to what was *really* bothering us. This process was often not a quick one. At times, we would need to go off by ourselves to think.

It took awhile to shift from focusing on the other person to focusing on ourselves and understanding our own intensity. Once we did, we would come back together to talk about the issue again—this time with an awareness of our own deeper feelings. Matt, at times, expressed feeling disrespected by my decisions; I often tapped into childhood feelings of not being listened to. Through the process we increased our understanding of each other.

I recognize now how unhealthy the pattern of conflict was that I experienced at home as a child. An angry tirade by my father and silence by my mother did nothing to further their relationship. I would surmise that the process probably kept both of them locked into a pattern of blaming the other person.

The gift conflict gives us is the opportunity to learn both about the other person and ourselves. There is a reason why we are reacting so strongly to the other person's words or actions. They are touching into a "hot spot" that we have within us. If we take the time to shift our focus from the other person to ourselves, to ask ourselves, "What is *really* bothering me about this issue?" we empower ourselves to resolve the issue in a positive manner. If we don't, we stay locked in perpetual conflict.

I learned a great deal about conflict by going through this experience with Matt. I can see now that the reason Matt and I were able to be so straightforward with each other was because, on a deep level, we felt safe with each other. Both he and I knew that the other person was committed to the relationship; that we were loved and wouldn't be abandoned. I am very grateful to Matt for giving me a safe place to learn this important lesson.

honesty on a daily basis

When we first began working on changing the level of honesty in our marriage, both Tom and I felt threatened at being so emotionally vulnerable with each other. We each worried that if the other person got to *really* know us, they would disapprove and pull away. We discovered the opposite to be true. When we began being more honest with each other, we began to feel much more connected. We had much more of a sense of genuinely knowing the other person.

I have found that it is a constant challenge to be open and honest. It is a daily commitment. When Tom asks me if something is bothering me I try to truthfully answer, "Yes" if there is, and tell him about it, or "Yes, but I'm not ready to talk about it yet." In years past, I would have replied, "No" then been angry that he hadn't continued to ask.

One of the biggest challenges facing a relationship is to stay in touch with each other. Even when two people live in the same house, a fear of emotional intimacy can cause couples to co-exist rather than truly connect. Tom and I have found that it is very important to work on this consistently. When we lapse into a pattern of not making the effort to connect on a deeper emotional level, we can tell a definite difference in our relationship. We become dissatisfied.

One of the most effective ways for Tom and I to maintain our communication is by taking walks together. When we are outside we are better able to focus on each other because we leave behind the everyday distractions. There are no phones to be answered, no television or computer to compete with. It is very calming just to be out in nature.

We make it a point on these walks to go beyond daily business conversation such as, "We need to make an appointment to get the car serviced." Instead, we take these opportunities to say, "How are you doing? How are you feeling about things?"

When Tom and I stay emotionally open to each other on a regular basis, we find that we both feel a greater sense of satisfaction within the relationship. Almost always, if we start to feel discontent, it is because we have not taken the time (or had the courage) to be emotionally connected. Maintaining true emotional intimacy is a process that requires courage, commitment, and persistence.

being gentle with ourselves

Sometimes honesty is gut-wrenchingly hard. It is an absolute necessity for us to learn to be gentle with ourselves as we take steps to becoming more truthful. If we don't, we risk overwhelming ourselves and stopping the process.

When I initially received spiritual guidance to begin this writing, I was doing so for no one other than myself. I found the process to be very helpful for me. It challenged me to clarify my beliefs and gave me a purpose for rereading old journals. I was within my comfort zone.

That changed dramatically when I started feeling guided to put the random sections I had typed into book form for others to read. Deep, gut-wrenching fears surfaced. I had lived much of my life in secrecy and the thought of being so incredibly open and vulnerable brought up great anxiety.

The only way I could proceed with the writing was to keep an open notebook on the desk beside me. In it, I wrote all of the fears that surfaced. I had to get them outside of myself. I wrote page after page of "worst case" scenarios that I was sure would occur if I were to ever publish a book telling the truth about both my brother's suicide and my own personal struggles. I was convinced that I would be disowned by my family for speaking so publicly about the suicide that we had kept secret for more than 30 years.

After writing the second draft of this book, I put it aside. It was 18 months before I was once again ready to proceed with it. During those 18 months, I continued to feel a great deal of anxiety at the thought of being so open about my experiences.

I worked on understanding why the truth held so much fear for me. I came to the realization that the core issue was my fear of abandonment. I was deeply concerned about the fact that my beliefs differed significantly from those held by most of my family members. I felt fearful that in order to be myself—to really state my beliefs when they contrasted so much with the beliefs of others—I would risk losing their love.

It has been a challenge for me to work through these fears. I think the turning point came when I started to realize how very healing the process of writing and talking about my brother's suicide has been for me. I am far more at peace with it now than I have ever been before. I find myself much more able to forgive both Norm—and myself—for what took place.

If I had not been able to be gentle with myself, to give myself the time I needed, I would never have gotten to the point of being able to speak the truth so publicly. I realize now that this journey toward honesty has involved literally hundreds of baby steps. I am grateful for each and every one of them.

lesson 7

it helps when we understand the process of growth

Continuous effort—not strength or intelligence—is the key to unlocking our potential. Persistence will reward us with results far greater than we had ever envisioned.

Author unknown

Life is messy. There's just no way around it. As much as we would like it to be light and fun and clear-cut all the time, that's just not the way it is.

Some of the time, no matter how I work to become enlightened, it seems like I'm walking through mud. I will have a disagreement with my husband about our household budget, and life gets messy; I will unintentionally hurt a loved one's feelings, and life gets messy; I will realize that I still react to unresolved issues from my childhood, and life gets messy. Often, when I feel out-of-sorts, I don't even know why.

I don't know where I ever got the idealistic notion that life wasn't supposed to be messy. I spent many years thinking that the reason I felt confusion, pain, and frustration was because I was defective—that somehow other people didn't experience these things.

As a child, I watched "Father Knows Best" and "The Donna Reed Show" on TV and I believed that was how the rest of the world lived. I believed that in everyone else's homes little girls were cherished by their fathers, money was never a concern, and there was never conflict in the family.

It was only as I got older, and had open conversations with friends and acquaintances, that I came to realize that no one grows up in a perfect, TV family. We all struggle at times. We all are faced with challenges.

growth is a life-long process

When I was 21 years old and newly married, I looked at my mother-in-law (who was 45 years old at the time) as being a finished project. She seemed so complete. She appeared so sure of herself and her beliefs. As I approached the age of 45 myself, I gained an entirely different perspective. I began to realize that we don't ever get finished—that growing and changing is a lifelong endeavor.

When I was younger, I viewed people in their 40s and 50s as pieces of cement. I thought they were fully formed and remained constant. It has been a startling revelation to me to realize that this belief is not at all accurate. People are much more like rivers—constantly flowing and bending to adapt to new insights and experiences.

I now understand that *each* age brings with it new growth opportunities. It has been inspiring to me to see my mother-in-law, now in her 70s and facing health concerns, explore new attitudes and healing methods. Each stage of our life holds a wealth of new lessons for us if we are only open to them.

taking responsibility for ourselves

In my experience, taking responsibility for ourselves is a necessity if we want to improve our life. I had a conversation with an acquaintance recently. She told me, in great detail, about her life: coming from a very dysfunctional family; being raped as a teenager; being physically abused in one of her three marriages; the extreme difficulty she experiences now in developing female friendships.

This woman expressed great pain, and spoke of the anger and bitterness she holds inside. When I suggested that she seek counseling to work through and heal these issues, she said, "That's not for me. Spending so much time on yourself is selfish." I left that conversation feeling sad for this intelligent, vivacious woman who views herself as a victim. In doing so, she is resigning herself to a lifetime of unhappiness.

Many people face trauma in their lives. If we come from a strong pattern of seeing ourselves as victims, we will most likely assume there is nothing that can be done about the emotional pain that accompanies these experiences. If, however, we can entertain an attitude of being empowered, we will recognize that we *do* have a choice; that we *can* do something about the emotional turmoil that we feel.

As we go through difficult experiences in life, the question for each of us to ask ourselves is whether or not we are willing to take the steps required to release the pain. We can choose to face the issues and heal, or we can carry them around for the rest of our lives.

I know from personal experience how very difficult the healing process can be. It takes great courage to be willing to look deeply within ourselves—to feel the feelings and make the necessary changes in our life. That is why M. Scott Peck, M.D. refers to the growth process in his bestseller as "the road less traveled." I also know, however, that it is the journey we must undertake if we wish to feel true inner peace and well-being.

living consciously

One of the steps I needed to take on my own healing journey was to learn how to live consciously. By that I mean developing the ability to stand back and observe myself—my thoughts and my actions.

We have all developed patterns of behavior—ways of thinking about, and reacting to, situations in our lives. When we are not consciously aware of these patterns, they become our "default" settings…those that we revert back to without even being aware of them. Our patterns affect every area of our lives, including relationships with others and our relationship with ourselves.

Once we begin to live consciously, we are able to step back from our lives and see them from a larger perspective. Our goal is to gain an objective understanding of our thoughts and actions so we can recognize the impact they have on our lives.

If, for example, we have a history of unhealthy friendships, we can view it in two ways. One would be to feel we are victims and complain to anyone who will listen about how we have been wronged.

A second, more empowered way would be to stand back and observe, "I have had three friends in a row that have borrowed money from me and not repaid it, then ended the relationship. What are these experiences trying to teach me about friendship and the type of people I choose for friends? Am I trying to 'buy' my friends' affections by loaning them money? Do I need to work on having healthier boundaries with my friends?"

We have the ability to change our patterns. We are not destined to react to a situation in the same way we would have in the past. When we take the time to examine our patterns, we take our actions from the realm of the unconscious to the conscious. In doing so, we empower ourselves to live in a more satisfying manner.

Observing our actions and our thoughts is a skill that is learned gradually. The goal is awareness. If you have lived many years in a relatively unaware state, this will probably seem very unfamiliar at first.

Above all, be gentle with yourself. Instead of being critical with yourself for reacting the way you did to a situation, stand back for a change. Objectively view your reaction. Ask yourself, for example,

"Why *did* I react with such anger? What was *really* going on for me?" The more accustomed we become to observing ourselves without judgment, the more likely we are to change the patterns and behaviors we don't like.

As we practice this objectivity we take the first step in seeing a larger view of our lives. If we step back even further we are able to ask ourselves even more meaningful spiritual questions — "Why is this situation in my life at all? What is it my soul wants to learn?" These questions remind us that there is great purpose to the experiences in our lives.

Without the willingness to be objective, we often miss the significance of a situation. We are so busy pointing fingers at others that we miss the real opportunity for growth. As long as we are blaming others (or fate), we are relegating ourselves to the role of victim. If, instead, we turn the spotlight on ourselves and ask what our part is in the situation—what our pattern is and the lesson we need to learn—we then become empowered.

If we are willing to do the work necessary to understand our own patterns and motivations, we free ourselves to have healthier, happier relationships. If we don't do the work, we will probably create the same situation (or a similar one) over and over again until our soul learns the lesson it needs.

gaining objectivity

Gaining objectivity about our feelings and patterns can be very challenging. There are probably an endless number of techniques for accomplishing the task. Some of the methods I use on a regular basis are:

- *"Checking in" with myself*—If I am agitated about a situation, I will pause and try to understand what is bothering me. If I am in a room full of people I will try to find a space off by myself (restrooms work well) where I can take several deep breaths and gain a different perspective on the experience. Sometimes that "time out" will be sufficient to see the situation with more clarity.

- *Viewing the situation as though it was happening to someone else*— This is a technique I have found especially helpful. I will think of a friend—someone whom I really admire—and think about how they would view, or handle, the situation. It is much easier for me, in this way, to understand the dynamics of the issue without judging either it or myself.

- *Journaling*—If the issue I am dealing with is larger, or especially complex, I often turn to journaling. I have found this process to be invaluable in gaining a larger perspective on issues. Sometimes I will gain clarity right away. Sometimes I will need to journal on a number of different occasions about the same topic, usually writing about a different aspect of it each time. Many times I have completed the journaling, moved on to a different activity, and then had a spark of insight into the issue I was writing about. Journaling helps me release the emotion I have regarding a situation so that I can view it from a different vantage point.

- *Processing with friends*—Friends and loved ones can be an invaluable source of insight for us, provided their intention is to be as objective as possible and encourage our growth instead of our victimization. If they know us well, they probably know some of our patterns better than we do, and can help us gain meaningful insight.

- *Meditating*—If I am reacting to a situation with considerable agitation, it is helpful for me to take a few minutes to meditate. What I most often need is an opportunity to acknowledge my "inner child" and the hurt, confusion, and fear she is feeling. I envision myself as a young child safely cradled in strong, supportive arms. From this perspective it is easier for me to understand why the issue is so painful to me. I become the observer—not making judgments, just observations. The more I can accept the fact that there are issues that cause me confusion and pain, the more I am able to accept myself and set about loving myself into wholeness.

layer by layer

I have often been amazed at the process of growth in my life. It will seem to me that I have handled an issue: I've looked at it, written about it, discussed it with friends, prayed about it, etc. I've arrived at a point where I even feel like I have come to terms with it. Then—a few months, or a year, or several years later—it reappears (sometimes with as much power as it had originally).

I have come to realize that growth does not occur in a linear fashion. Instead, the process of growth reminds me of the peeling of an onion. I peel a layer, and at a later date, another layer presents itself. Each time this happens I am in a slightly different place in my life and have the opportunity to view the issue from a different perspective. Because of this, the healing of an issue occurs at a deeper level each time.

I have found that the challenge of this process lies in not becoming discouraged when a new layer appears. When we understand that issues may contain many layers, we are more able to be gentle with ourselves. If, instead, we judge ourselves negatively—"I thought I handled this before; I must have been kidding myself"—we prolong the process.

treating ourselves with gentleness

I have come to the conclusion that healing, for me, is facilitated by love, not judgment. Being critical of myself has rarely, if ever, helped me work through a problem. I am reminded of my son's seventh grade basketball coach, who told the team that they were the worst team he had ever coached. I was appalled. Did he really think that statement would motivate the team? I never saw any evidence that it helped the players.

Instead, I think it encouraged them to think of themselves as losers.

I can't recall ever having flourished under the guidance of someone who didn't take the time to recognize my strengths. When I look back at my life, I know without a doubt that the times I grew most were when I had the encouragement of someone who believed I could accomplish the task—even if *I* didn't think I could; someone who took the time to look into my eyes with a quiet, unwavering belief that I would accomplish the challenge. It is that same support that we most need from ourselves. It is something that I am learning to give myself as an adult. It requires a whole new pattern of thinking.

our capacity to grow

I believe deeply in the capacity of human beings to grow and change at any stage of life. I am a very different person now than I was in my 20s. I am much more willing to consider new ideas and thoughts. In fact, I have an inner drive to do so. Many of my beliefs, attitudes, and perspectives have changed and for this I am immensely grateful.

Although my growth oftentimes doesn't come easily, it is definitely worthwhile. Making these changes has brought about so much more contentment in my life, so much more peace. I am filled with hope for the future. The path to wholeness is certainly not the easiest road to take, but it is definitely the most rewarding.

lesson 8

we get there by taking one step at a time

Be not afraid of growing slowly—only of standing still.

Chinese proverb

I have realized with the same surprise, time and again throughout my life, that, having looked at a far and frightening prospect and been dismayed, I can cope with it after all by remembering the simple lesson I learned so long ago. I remind myself to look not at the rocks far below but at the first small and relatively easy step and, having taken it, to take the next one, feeling a sense of accomplishment with each move, until I have done what I wanted to do, gotten where I wanted to be, and can look back, amazed and proud of the distance I have come.

Author unknown

My journey toward discovering my self-worth has been long and frequently very frustrating. I have had so much to learn and so many things to change. In the beginning I felt like I was a mess and that I didn't really know how to start. I oftentimes felt very discouraged and overwhelmed. I wanted the process of growth to be black and white: you take this course, do the homework, and at the end of the semester you are healed. Unfortunately, there is no such prepackaged course. In reality, we continually develop it for ourselves.

In looking back, I can more easily understand why it felt so overwhelming. I needed to make changes not only mentally and emotionally, but spiritually and physically as well. I explained it to a relative once by saying, "What you don't understand about me is that I just want to feel better. It's as simple as that. I don't want to be in pain anymore." That pretty much summed it up.

taking baby steps

One of my favorite movies is *What About Bob?* because it is both fun and profound at the same time. In it, Bill Murray plays Bob, a multi-phobic patient whose psychologist (Richard Dreyfuss) has written a bestseller entitled *Baby Steps*. Bob believes that this new technique can heal him and, therefore, goes to great lengths to follow his psychologist on vacation. Throughout the movie Bob reminds himself, "baby steps!" each time he is confronted with something that terrifies him.

The first time I watched the movie I thought how powerful that message truly was. I had been learning the exact same lesson in my own life: that to deal with frightening issues, I often had to proceed by taking baby steps…first one step, then another, then yet another. Eventually I would see that I really *was* making progress.

The good news is that a person doesn't have to do *all* the work before they start to feel better. As I took my steps, one after the other, I started to realize that I was feeling a bit lighter inside; a bit less weighed down emotionally.

After working on certain issues, like learning how to have more emotionally intimate relationships, and coming to terms with my brother's suicide, I felt significant change. I felt so much lighter and brighter *on the inside*—as though I had put down a dark, heavy object

I had been carrying. With each of my baby steps the quality of my life improves and for this I am very grateful.

the first step—make the choice to heal your life

Our *intention* to heal is incredibly important. It is that intention that separates those who ultimately will do the work from those who will carry their emotional pain around for the rest of their lives. A sincere intention to heal leads us to action. It is the difference between sitting around complaining about a problem and taking the steps necessary to solve it.

Our intention generates the *perseverance* we will need to heal. After a while, when we have successfully made changes in our attitudes and in our lives, the motivation gets a lot easier. We begin to feel better. We have successes under our belt. We have proven to ourselves that we have the power to change our life, and that feels exciting.

the second step—identify a particular problem

In hindsight, it seems that the lessons I needed to learn simply presented themselves in the course of daily living. An issue would become particularly agitating or painful, and I would realize that was what I needed to concentrate on. Sometimes the problem felt very generalized —"I feel depressed." Other times I knew more specifically what I was dealing with—"I feel such anger about the way I am being treated in this situation!" When we take the time to listen to ourselves, and acknowledge a problem, we are taking a vitally important step toward identifying the lesson we need to learn.

the third step—ask for guidance

Spirit wants you to heal and supports you in your healing. I have found that the most effective way to progress toward healing in any situation is to turn to Spirit and ask for guidance. I ask to be shown the person or thing that can best facilitate my healing. I ask that the process be for my highest good. I then trust that the appropriate book/person/seminar/counselor, etc. will be shown to me.

I have come to have great faith in this process because it has proven itself to be true so many times in my life. After making the request, I will pay special attention to the things that present themselves to me: I may hear a particular counselor's name mentioned several times; I will receive a flyer telling of a seminar or class dealing with the issue I am working on; I will be guided to a book that will enable me to work on the issue myself.

Spirit has many ways of communicating with us. Ask and be patient. You *will* be shown.

the fourth step—take action

Once you have been guided to the therapist, the book, the class, the seminar, etc., it is time for action. I know how terribly frightening this can be. As I drove to my first counseling session years ago, I was filled with fear. What if the therapist didn't think I was "sick" enough and said I was wasting her time? Or worse yet, what if she *did* think I was "sick" enough to need therapy? Either prospect terrified me.

I now realize that it wasn't a matter of being "sick." When the therapist listened to my story, she heard my pain and set about helping me to heal it. I am deeply grateful that I took those first steps. In hindsight, it was an incredibly brave and loving thing to do for myself.

being gentle to ourselves

Our steps toward healing involve facing the truth of what doesn't work in our life and then changing it: whether it is an erroneous belief, a childhood pattern, or a way of relating to others or ourselves. In most instances, we have held these attitudes and patterns for many years.

I have found that it is of the utmost importance to be gentle with myself while I am trying to make changes. If I become critical and perfectionistic with myself, I feel discouraged and find it twice as hard to make the shift. As psychologist Dr. Phil McGraw says, "When young children first learn to walk, they stand up, take a few tentative steps, then fall down. Do we go to them and say, 'Get up, you dumb baby!'? No, we give them the time they need to learn this new skill." We are just the same. We are learning new skills.

It is particularly important in those times when we are struggling to whisper to ourselves, "You can do this. I know you can. You just need to take baby steps."

freeing ourselves to fly

Some time ago, I was searching for an analogy to explain my healing process to my husband. The thought came to me that it was as though I had spent most of my life in the basket of a hot air balloon that just couldn't rise. Heavy ropes had anchored me to the ground. As I have taken my steps toward healing, I have cut those ropes one at a time (often with a great deal of hard work), and now the balloon is beginning to rise. After spending so much time tethered to the ground, it is incredibly exciting to begin to fly!

lesson 9

we create our reality

Attitudes—

Words can never adequately convey the incredible impact of our attitude toward life. The longer I live the more convinced I become that life is 10 percent what happens to us and 90 percent how we respond to it.

I believe the single most significant decision I can make on a day-to-day basis is my choice of attitude. It is more important than my past, my education, my bankroll, my successes or failures, fame or pain, what other people think of me or say about me, my circumstances, or my position. Attitude keeps me going or cripples my progress. It alone fuels my fire or assaults my hope. When my attitudes are right, there's no barrier too high, no valley too deep, no dream too extreme, no challenge too great for me.

Charles Swindoll

We create our reality. We do this in many ways. One of the ways we do this is through our attitude. The concept of creating our reality is one that I struggled with for a very long time. I had a very difficult time grasping it. For those of us who grew up strongly viewing ourselves as victims, it is a particularly unfamiliar idea to wrestle with.

I was accustomed to viewing life as something that happened *to* me; not something I had a hand in creating. Bit by bit, though, I started to entertain the notion that my thoughts and attitudes did affect the quality of my life. I began observing other people, their beliefs, and their lives.

The conclusion I came to was that their attitudes had more than just a subtle effect upon their lives; their attitudes had a huge impact.

victim vs. co-creator

One of the most basic ways we affect our lives is in the way we interpret our place in the scheme of things. If we view ourselves as insignificant beings without a great deal of worth, we probably are more likely to think we are victims—powerless and at the mercy of the world.

If, on the other hand, we gain an awareness of ourselves as divine beings working **with** God, it makes all the difference. Instead of being *reactive*, we become *proactive*. We examine the way we live our lives— our beliefs and actions—and see if they are bringing us the quality of life that we desire. We start to understand that we have much more power than we ever thought we did.

If you are not sure of how you view yourself, the best way to find out is to become an observer, paying attention to the words you say and the things you think. When your lottery ticket numbers *aren't* drawn, do you say to yourself, "That figures. If I didn't have bad luck I wouldn't have any luck at all!" When you are having trouble with others do you think, "What's the use of talking to them about it? They're not going to listen to me anyway!" Do you constantly find yourself blaming other people? Is it always *their* fault when things go wrong? Sometimes listening to ourselves can be an eye-opener, and that's a wonderful place to begin.

how do we see life?

Anaïs Nin, a French-American writer, said very succinctly: "We don't see things as they are. We see them as *we* are." The first time I came across that quote, I had absolutely no idea what the author was talking about. I remembered this quote from time to time, however, and found it coming to my awareness in different situations.

In the beginning, I would find myself pondering the quote in reference to someone else. I wasn't objective enough at that point to see it clearly in my own life. Many times I would listen to a friend or relative tell about a frustrating experience. If I knew them well, I would often think to myself, "Of course they would view the situation that way. It touches into their issue of..." Sometimes, if I knew both parties involved, I would hear about the experience from both points of view and see how incredibly different they could be.

Years ago my husband and I watched the "Dick VanDyke" show. In one episode Rob (Dick VanDyke) tells his co-workers about how unreasonable his wife, Laura, had been the night before. He describes the experience in great detail and, as he does, we see the experience through his eyes. Rob comes home from work, tuxedo-clad and in a playful, joyful mood. Laura appears unkempt and cranky. Despite Rob's best efforts he can't improve her mood and the evening ends in a huge argument.

In the next scene we see Laura speaking with her best friend, Millie. Laura is likewise agitated about the experience and tells Millie her side of the story. Again we are shown the previous evening, this time through Laura's eyes. When Rob comes home from work in a foul mood she greets him in a ball gown. Despite her best efforts to be cheerful and loving, his bad temper eventually leads them into the argument.

In the third scene we are shown what *really* took place that evening: both of them a bit off-center and grumpy, both contributing to the ensuing argument.

I have remembered that episode for so many years because I thought there was such great truth in it. Oftentimes, we aren't trying to tell our story inaccurately; it's just that the way we perceived the situation was so different from how the other person saw it, or how it really happened. We viewed it through the filter of our *own* issues and the other person did the same.

One of our challenges is to learn to recognize our own issues so that we can view situations more objectively. If we aren't aware of our issues, we will continue to see the world through them, as if looking through colored glass. If we feel we are unlovable, for example, we may interpret people's expressions of love for us as insincere. If we believe people to be untrustworthy, we will probably view business transactions with an exaggerated feeling of skepticism. If we are highly critical of ourselves, we will most likely find constant fault with others.

turning the spotlight on ourselves

If you find that you are unhappy with what you are experiencing in the world, the best thing you can do is to turn the spotlight off of others and onto yourself. Empower yourself. Instead of approaching life from a victim mode ("They are doing this *to* me"), explore looking at the issue from a viewpoint of, "What am *I* doing to create this situation in my life?" and ask, "What do I need to learn from this?"

When we look at life from this larger, expanded viewpoint we are then in a position to *change* what it is we no longer want in our life. We are in a position to release the belief/attitude/action that contributed to the situation to begin with. And, as we adopt new attitudes that would be more helpful to us, we see our life transforming in a new, positive direction. We start to become the kind of person we truly wish to be. We are then on our way to creating happier, more fulfilling experiences.

lesson 10

a good support system is priceless

A friend is a person with whom you dare to be yourself.

Frank Crane

One of the best gifts I have ever given myself is the gift of being open to friendship. I have found this to be vital in my growth process. Early on I realized that if I aspired to lead a conscious, self-loving, empowered life, it would be necessary for me to surround myself with friends and family members who would encourage and support these characteristics in me, and value these qualities in their own lives.

As I worked at developing healthier attitudes, I brought into my life friends who were likewise working very hard on their own growth. I was very grateful to have these souls in my life. I realized that it would have been twice as hard for me to change if I surrounded myself with people who encouraged my previous victim mentality.

I have spent numerous hours in conversation with friends, discussing new attitudes and how they were applicable in our lives. In a world that is so quick to discount the spiritual, it has been very important for me to be able to share my experiences and ideas in a safe environment, knowing that they would be treated with respect.

These conversations have also given me many opportunities to better understand my own emotional firestorms. When an issue was particularly upsetting to me, a friend would listen patiently. Later, when

I had released some of the emotion, my friend would compassionately say, "If you had created this, why do you think you would have done so?" That question, lovingly asked, would help me come to a larger, more grounded, spiritual perspective on the matter.

we are continually supported

It truly amazes me how the process of life works. In hindsight, I realize that a number of people have come into my life at the time when they were most needed. I believe that this is one way Spirit supports our growth.

One friend, years ago, was in my life for about two years until she moved out of state and we grew apart. I don't think the friendship was meant to last longer than it did; I think we were both ready to move on. She played a vital role in my life while she was with me, though, for she was the one who led me to therapy. She shared with me the fact that she had previously gone to counseling and told me how very much the process had helped her. I will be forever grateful to her for helping me overcome my fears of seeking professional help.

There have been so many people who have acted as signposts along my journey, helping me find my way. They have often given me insights or modeled characteristics that I wanted to develop. As I look back, I see the divine roles they have played in my growth and I honor them.

going into the storm

Several years ago Tom and I rented a cottage with my sister for a week. One evening a storm approached in the distance over the lake and the huge dark clouds beckoned my sister and me outside for a closer look. Tom and the children were safely ensconced in the cottage, and he was concerned about our wanting to go outside. Knowing how determined we were to do it, he said in a very serious tone, "Okay. But if you go outside, hold hands." My sister Marlene and I burst out laughing. Tom's concern and warmth were so evident in his humor.

I have often thought of Tom saying this and have come to the conclusion that holding hands epitomizes mankind at its best. It symbolizes the support humans are capable of offering each other. We would be wise to follow Tom's advice throughout all the experiences in our lives—not just the storms.

lesson 11

our identity is our responsibility

The golden opportunity you are seeking is in yourself. It is not in your environment; it is not in luck or chance, or the help of others; it is in yourself alone.

Orison Swett Marden

When Tom and I got married, I was 21 and he was 22. When I look back at pictures of those first few years, a wave of empathy and compassion comes over me. We were both so young and knew so little about ourselves and the workings of the world. We were so very naïve.

In hindsight, I now realize how unrealistic my attitudes were about marriage. I completely believed all the fairy tales I had been told as a child. I believed a prince would come and rescue me and we would live happily ever after. Only we didn't. Even though I married a man I loved deeply—my prince—he didn't "make me" feel better; he didn't take away the pain I felt inside.

For a long time I resented him for that. I was somehow sure that he had the ability, but just wasn't willing to do it. I became angry with him for not reading my mind and knowing what I wanted (when I was certain he had the ability to do so). The angrier that I felt toward him, the more alienated I felt from him.

"and the two shall be as one"

When Tom and I married in the early '70s, an emphasis was put on two people becoming as one when they wed. I took this literally. I viewed Tom and myself as two halves of one entity. I clearly remember thinking that Tom and I together, with our complementary strengths, made up "one heck of a person."

As incredible as this may sound, it wasn't until my late 30s that I woke up to the realization that we were *each* supposed to be a whole person! I began to understand that it was *my responsibility* to develop goals and dreams for my life. This was a total reorientation of the way I viewed myself. At first it was very, very uncomfortable. It was such a large responsibility and I didn't know if I was up to the task!

As I struggled to understand who I was as a separate entity from my husband, I began to see him more objectively. It slowly began to dawn on me that I had been angry with him for things that he never had control over to begin with. It *wasn't* that he didn't want to make me feel good early in our marriage; it was that he never had the power to do so. The emotional pain I felt existed within myself. If I were to ever feel better, *I* had to take responsibility for healing the pain.

gaining a larger perspective

As I learned more about metaphysics and spirituality, I developed a different outlook on my life. I began to understand that I have come into this incarnation to experience exactly what I am experiencing. I chose it on a soul level. It is the perfect (though often not easy!) way for my soul to learn what it needs to learn.

Once I started understanding this, it gave me a different perspective on my marriage. Tom wasn't responsible for my growth; I was. For me to resent him for my not feeling good was unfair; it was an unconscious way of not taking responsibility for my own life. As long as I believed it was *his* job, I didn't have to do it. Holding this attitude perpetuated my belief that I was a victim and kept me feeling powerless.

looking at it differently

Having been married more than 30 years now, I look at things very differently. I understand that many people enter into marriage thinking that their spouse is going to make them whole. If we don't move past that belief, however, we limit our own lives. We miss the fact that our growth is *our* responsibility and that we are here to serve a divine purpose. To the degree that we perceive ourselves as victims—as unable to be whole on our own—we handicap ourselves.

For someone who had spent a lifetime defining herself in terms of her relationship to others—my parents' daughter, Tom's wife, Mandy and Matt's mother, my nieces' and nephews' aunt—this was a major shift in consciousness. I found it to be both frightening and empowering.

When I started to grasp the fact that I was *already* a whole person and had a unique contribution to make to the world, I began to think differently about myself. I began to honor myself more. I began to realize that I was valuable and did want to fulfill the purposes for which I had incarnated.

listening to society's messages

I do not think that it is easy to grow up in modern-day society and still retain an awareness of our basic divine nature. So many of the messages we receive tell us that our worth is dependent upon *external* factors: a prestigious career, a new car, an abundance of money. Women, for example, are given the message that their value depends on their body size. They are led to believe that they are unacceptable if they do not possess the waif-like appearance of a model.

The best way we can counteract these inaccurate messages is to stand back and look at them. By taking a step back, we become more objective and realize that these messages are *not* rooted in truth; they are rooted in commercialism.

It is often deeply challenging to remember who we *really* are. It isn't until we view ourselves and our lives from a much larger perspective that we understand the truth that each of us is a *divine* being who has come to earth for *divine* purposes.

Once we begin to view our life from this larger, more enlightened vantage point, we change the way we think about ourselves. We begin to develop a deeper appreciation for who we are. We begin to take responsibility for our own lives. We begin to release the false notion that we are victims. And we begin to understand that the messages of the world are not accurate and that we do not have to believe them.

coming home to ourselves

For many of us, learning to go within and get in touch with ourselves on a deeper level is somewhat (maybe even *very*) frightening. We're not sure of what we are going to find. Oftentimes, the state of disconnection within ourselves is so severe that we don't even know where to begin. If we are brave, really brave, we take a baby step. Then another. Then another.

As we take these steps we start to become more comfortable with both the process and ourselves. We begin to see ourselves differently. We begin to recognize our strengths and become less fearful of the dragons that we thought resided within us. We begin to see that those dragons were really just pain and that, once acknowledged, they start to disappear. We begin to actually *like* the persons we are and create more time to get to know ourselves.

As we take these steps in coming home to ourselves, we begin to see ourselves as empowered instead of powerless. We accept the responsibility of healing ourselves and creating our own happiness. We begin to understand that we *are* up to the task. And then, if we should choose to share our life with another person, it will be out of our strength—not neediness. We will truly be inviting people to *share* in our growth rather than asking them to be responsible for it.

lesson 12

making peace with a parent
sets both of you free

One of the most powerful and pervasive attitudes regarding childhood in our culture is the idea that at some point you cease to be a child and are an adult forever after. This is completely contrary to the facts of emotional growth and development, resulting in much confusion and often severe, unnecessary self-contempt in adults.

W. Hugh Missildine, M.D.

My father and I had a difficult relationship while I was growing up. He had experienced a harsh childhood and had grown up to be stern, controlling, and emotionally distant. *His* way was the way things were to be done. It appeared to me that he viewed his role as consisting of feeding, clothing, and setting a good moral example for his children. Emotional nurturing and the daily raising of children fell to my mother.

My father found safety in facts and figures and avoided conversations that dealt with affection or feelings. I, on the other hand, was a very sensitive young girl who longed for her father to love her—to take an interest in her life, to show her that she had value. I felt that I wasn't nearly as important to him as his job.

By the time I became a teenager, I was deeply angry. I resented the way he talked *at* me, never **with** me. I resented that my thoughts and feelings didn't seem to matter at all to him. My mother chose the route of passivity in dealing with my father. I chose a different course and stood up to him. Because of that, he and I had many angry arguments during my teenage years.

After my mother died, my father stopped speaking of her. It was as though she had never existed at all. It was the same situation that had occurred five years earlier with the death of my brother.

Eight months after my mother's death, I attended a Christmas get-together at the home of my father's new lady friend. It was the first Christmas that my mother wasn't with us and it was a terribly painful time. My dad and my future stepmother were married the next summer.

I changed toward my father after my mother passed away. Instead of being feisty with him, as I had been as a teenager, I shut down. Instead of expressing my anger, I swallowed what I wanted to say. Without the security of my mother's presence, I no longer felt safe to be truthful with him, so I began to keep my distance and limited the number of times I was with him.

I continued to be frustrated with our relationship. I wanted so much more than he could give. I wanted to have an emotional connection and conversations that didn't involve his job. I wanted to know that he loved me and that I wasn't just "one of the kids." I wanted him to address me by name instead of referring to me as "girl" and introducing me as "daughter number two." I rarely saw him or spoke to him outside of family gatherings. We continued this emotionally distant relationship for the next 25 years.

a turning point

Sometimes, in hindsight, I am able to clearly see that Spirit has been at work in my life. One of those times was when a dear friend suggested I read a book entitled *Your Inner Child of the Past* by W. Hugh Missildine, M.D. This book helped me take a very significant step toward improving my relationship with my father. It helped me to do what I had previously been unable to do—to look at our relationship in a more objective way.

In his book, Dr. Missildine, a child psychiatrist, tells of observing both children and adults as they struggled with their problems. He began to see the correlation between particular attitudes and demands of parents, and the development of troublesome patterns in children.

Dr. Missildine also observed that each of us, from adolescence on, carries within ourselves our "inner child of the past"—a set of feelings and attitudes brought from childhood. (These are formed largely by the family attitudes and emotional atmosphere of our early childhood.)

In a literal sense, our childhood exists within us now. As we grow into adults, the patterns we established when we were young continue to affect everything we do and feel. They even influence our current relationships with friends, colleagues, spouses, and our own children.

on a personal level

As I read Dr. Missildine's book, I began to understand the patterns that existed in my own childhood. I also started to see how these patterns were still playing themselves out in my adult life. It was as though I had created a set of audiotapes as a child and was still playing them back on a daily basis—this time through my own internal dialogues. I began to understand that I *hadn't* really left my childhood behind, even if I thought I had. It was alive and thriving in my attitudes and feelings.

I became aware of my inner child and started paying attention to how it asserted itself. I saw it surfacing when I reacted strongly to situations, when I felt rebellious, when I felt unsafe in any way. I gradually learned that it is the part of me that fears abandonment, that procrastinates, that becomes shy at times, and that feels insecure.

I also came to realize that my inner child is one of my most cherished parts of myself. It is the part of me that is creative, playful and loves to sing. It is the enthusiastic, joyful part of myself. My inner child loves soft fabrics and beautiful music, and wants to hug every puppy it sees.

The best way I found to get in touch with my inner child was to bring out old photos of myself when I was little. I keep one photo—taken when I was about 4 years old—framed and displayed in my home office. Seeing that sweet little face helps me get in touch with my childhood joys and frustrations. It helps remind me that she *still* exists within me today.

understanding our inner parents

As I began to recognize my inner child, I also began to see that there is a part of me that assumes the role of "parent" to this inner child. This parent is also based upon the messages I was given as a child. I observed within myself both a "critical parent" and a "nurturing parent."

My inner critical parent adopted the negative messages that I had received as a child from my church, my family, and society: strong messages of not doing things "the right way" and of not being good enough. As I began to pay more attention to the voice of my inner critical parent, I was amazed at its strength and its frequency. I no longer needed an adult from the past to point out my shortcomings; I now did it for myself.

I found that my critical parent was threatened by my inner child. Oftentimes, when my inner child came forth and wanted to be heard, I would find myself disowning it, ignoring it, and scolding it. My inner critical parent said, "You are all grown up now and should no longer have these childish feelings." By not acknowledging the child part of me, there was a constant tug-of-war. The child wanted to be listened to; the adult wanted the child silenced.

I also came to recognize that there existed a more accepting part of myself—a "nurturing parent." I discovered it to be the part of me that had internalized warm, loving, supportive comments when I was growing up. It is the part of me that is gentle and kind to myself. It acknowledges my feelings and recognizes my efforts.

gaining additional insight

Dr. Missildine's concepts were immensely helpful to me in two ways. First, they helped me gain an objective understanding of the patterns I had developed as a child. Second, they helped me understand the way in which I continue these patterns through my inner dialogues. They helped me to recognize that I now treat myself, as an adult, the way that adults treated me as a child.

As I started becoming more aware of the dynamics of inner dialogue, I was amazed at the degree to which it affected my life. I had heard the term "inner child" before reading Dr. Missildine's book, and had even used the term on occasion. I had never really understood, however, that it played such a significant role in our lives.

I came to realize that the relationship between my inner child, my critical parent, and my nurturing parent literally determined whether or not I felt at peace within myself. This was incredibly useful information for me.

my father's surgery

When my father was 84 years old, he needed to have hip-replacement surgery. Because of the work I had been doing on learning to listen to my inner child, I was better able to understand my reaction to a conversation we had the night before he entered the hospital.

He had called to tell me the details surrounding his hospital stay. When I hung up the phone after we spoke, I felt terribly sad. In my journal entry that evening I wrote:

> When I was talking with Dad tonight I realized that I feel incredibly vulnerable...too vulnerable...around him. I wanted to cry. It

occurred to me how very angry I am at him for not loving me the way I needed to be loved. I don't avoid him now because I don't care—I avoid him because being around him and talking to him reminds me of how very, very much I did care; of how very much I wanted him to approve of me and cherish me and think that I was special.

My father's surgery went well, but it necessitated his staying in a rehabilitation center more than two weeks. I spent a great deal of time visiting him.

Dad's convalescence was difficult for the entire family. He was incredibly frustrated with the situation and the more I tried to make things better, the worse things seemed to get. Feelings that I had suppressed for many years surfaced and were very uncomfortable for me. In the evenings, at home, I spent time journaling, meditating, and trying to understand my feelings.

One evening, when Tom and I were discussing my relationship with my father, Tom gently said to me, "Do you know that you act differently with your father than you do with just about anybody else? You are a mature woman with other people. With your dad, you are still a child." It was a "light bulb moment." Tom was completely correct! In my relationships with others, I was a grown woman. In my relationship with my father, I was 6 years old and still looking for his approval.

As I struggled through my father's convalescence, I asked a friend—a school counselor—if she could give me any insights into the situation. She recommended an excellent book—*Making Peace With Your Parents* by Harold H. Bloomfield, M.D.

Dr. Bloomfield's book became another valuable resource for me. It gave me a new perspective on parent/child relationships. For my entire life I had wanted a close relationship with my father. I had always thought, however, that *he* would have to change in order for that to take place. That belief left me feeling frustrated and powerless. I realized, in reading the book, that I was *not* powerless. I came to understand that *I* could impact our relationship by changing my perspective.

taking the steps

I have found that the road to changing long-held perspectives is neither smooth nor easy. It is something that takes a great deal of effort for me. I realized after Dad's surgery that if my goal was to build a meaningful relationship with him, then I needed to devote time and energy to it.

I started to visit my father on a weekly basis even though this wasn't always easy. In addition to living in different cities, we had a lifetime of issues and emotional distance between us. Oftentimes I was uncomfortable around him because of my patterns of being submissive and desperately wanting his approval.

After some of these visits I felt so frustrated and drained that I cried all the way home. Pain from feeling disrespected in the present unleashed a storehouse of similar feelings from the past.

I felt encouraged, however, by now understanding that there were steps that I *could* take to make myself feel better—things, in fact, that I *needed* to do. I hadn't known that before. The insight filled me with hope and determination to do all that I could.

I recognized that one of the most important steps I could take would be to acknowledge my inner child who still felt so wounded emotionally. I began seeking out additional sources and eventually progressed to working on exercises from John Bradshaw's *Homecoming*—a book that gives specific ideas for healing inner child issues.

During this time, I also kept a separate journal for the inner child work I was doing. After visits with my father, I wrote about my successes and my struggles. I included observations of how I acted around my father and why it was I acted that way. I wrote about how our being together made me feel and the steps that I needed to take to feel more empowered in his presence. I worked at giving voice to feelings that had been long suppressed.

Gradually I began to dismantle the wall of anger that I had built to protect myself emotionally. Over the years I must have felt that if I was angry with my father, and didn't let him into my heart, then I would no longer be disappointed or hurt. It wasn't because I didn't care…it was because I cared so deeply and felt so vulnerable. As I journaled, and cried, and worked through the inner child exercises, I began to release some of the pain that I had carried my entire lifetime.

getting to know my father

I worked on my relationship with my father very consciously. Each time I visited Dad, I prepared myself in the car on the way there. I would ask for divine guidance and healing in this relationship. I would affirm to Spirit (and myself) that it was my intention to love my father unconditionally.

As time went on, I began to see changes in both my father and myself. As I began to chip away at the wall of anger and resentment I had held, he seemed to make a subtle shift in his attitudes toward me as well. We began to establish a more connected relationship.

I began to realize that I had never fully brought myself to the relationship before. I had always been far too afraid of being hurt. Consequently I didn't show my dad who I really was. I didn't voice my preferences in any way for fear he would disapprove, and emotionally abandon me.

For the next three years I visited my father weekly. We would spend several hours together each time. I took him to visit relatives, to go grocery shopping as my stepmother's health began to deteriorate, and to run errands. We went out to lunch or dinner together. We spent many hours talking about his childhood and his interests.

During this time I started getting to know my father as a person— not just a parent. I learned more about the dynamics of his childhood and the patterns they created in him. I began to gain an understanding of *his* inner child and *his* inner parents.

I developed a deeper appreciation for the impact his mother's death (when he was only 4 years old) had on him. His descriptions of the demanding, unaffectionate grandparents who raised him helped me gain insight into both the models he had for parent/child relationships and the critical messages he had internalized when he was being raised by them.

I came to realize that my father parented my siblings and myself in the very best way he knew how. He worked hard to put a roof over our heads and food on the table. He made sure we went to church every Sunday and that we graduated from Catholic high schools.

I also learned that my father saw himself in an amazingly different manner than the way I knew him. He saw himself as having little power and as treating others very respectfully. On two occasions I built up the courage to talk with Dad about the difficult relationship we had when I was a teenager. Each time he denied any awareness of our having a stormy time together.

During one of those conversations I told him how very difficult our relationship had been for me. He was incredibly surprised by the revelation. Through his eyes, there had never been a problem.

The three years I spent visiting Dad were incredibly challenging for me, but also some of the best moments I had ever had with him. There were moments when we were together that are crystallized in my memory…moments when I would look at him and think, "I love you. I truly love you."

a new challenge

In September of 2000 my stepmother died from congestive heart failure. My father had been married to her for 27 years. They had experienced a challenging relationship, but when she passed, he was lost without her.

Dad's grief at having lost his wife—combined with his own failing health and his inability to work (he had been self-employed until just two years prior)—caused him to be very angry. It was extremely difficult for me to spend time with him as he reverted back to the patterns I experienced as a child. He vented his anger and frustration by being controlling and highly critical. It was emotionally draining for me to be around him.

One day, after a particularly uncomfortable visit with him, I found myself lingering before leaving for home. I felt guided to tell him how I truly felt, but couldn't imagine how I would ever summon the courage to do so. The thought that I needed to be honest with him was very insistent.

I surprised myself when I said, "Dad, I need to talk with you before I go home." He sat down, and I paused…not having the slightest idea how to proceed. I felt very fearful. I said a quick prayer pleading for divine guidance.

My father and I talked for the next 45 minutes. It was one of the most honest talks we had ever had with each other. I told him that I understood why he was angry and depressed but that he was taking it out on me. We cried together as he told me how deeply he missed my stepmother and how he felt he didn't have a reason to live now that he could no longer work.

I explained, in turn, how difficult it was for me to be around him when he was so critical. I told him truthfully that I didn't allow anyone else in my life to treat me with such disrespect, and that I didn't know why I had allowed him to do so. He very earnestly replied, "I never tried to hurt you. I didn't know you were sensitive."

Dad repeated those words several times during our conversation. I was floored by them. It took my breath away to realize that my father had not known I was sensitive; I consider it one of my most basic qualities.

When I left that evening, we hugged and I told my dad I loved him. He said the same to me. The conversation had been very healing—I believe for both of us.

I have no doubt that it was Spirit that so strongly directed me to have that conversation. It was the last one I would ever have with my father. The following week he had a massive stroke. He died two weeks later. It had been less than four months since my stepmother passed over.

my father's final days

When my father was taken to the emergency room following his stroke, he was critically ill. His heart was working at a greatly reduced capacity, his lungs were filling with fluid, and his eyes were swollen shut from the fall he had taken after the stroke. It was gut-wrenching to see him in this condition. Over the next few days my siblings and I were faced with painful decisions about his care.

After a week it was clear to all of us that Dad was never going to improve. We had him transferred to a hospice facility so that he could spend his final days as comfortably as possible.

During these last two weeks of his life, my father had family members with him almost all the time. His sons and daughters, their spouses, his grandchildren and great-grandchildren, extended family, and friends all came to say their good-byes. It was an emotional time for all of us.

In the midst of these difficult days I found there to be deeply meaningful moments. One afternoon, when I was alone with my father, sitting next to his bed, I reached over and held his hand. Although he was very weak, and unable to speak, he responded by holding my hand firmly. It was a deeply emotional experience for me. I felt as though we had both laid aside our personalities and differences and all that remained was love. It was such a sweet time that it hurt…knowing that it would be over all too soon. For two hours I remained there, holding hands with my father and quietly crying.

continuing the healing

As I now write these words, it has been two years—almost to the day—since my father passed over. Looking back to those last two weeks of his life, I am deeply grateful for the opportunity we had to set aside our differences and experience the love that we felt for each other. It was very healing for me and, I sense, equally as healing for him.

I have continued to actively work on my relationship with my father since he passed over. Because of the spiritual experiences I have had, I *know* that we don't die when our bodies do. We are just freed up to live as spirit. I deeply believe that in between lifetimes on earth we continue to work on our soul's progression.

I have had many conversations with my father since he passed over. While I don't actually hear his responses to me, I sense that he is listening. In fact, I fully believe he is. I have used this time to tell him all the things I felt I couldn't say to him before.

I tell my father about myself—my interests, my dreams, my struggles. I talk to him a great deal about our relationship and why it was so often painful for me. I tell him all the things I *wish* I could have told him when he was on earth. I have found these conversations to be extremely helpful. They are dissipating years of wanting to have deep, open conversations with my father but not knowing how to do so.

alternative methods

I have also explored other methods for releasing the anger and resentments that I harbored toward my father for so many years. One of them, a series of energy balancing treatments, helped me to arrive at a crucial insight.

During the last session—in what felt like a flash of enlightenment—it occurred to me that I had been resenting my father for not giving me something *that I had been unwilling to give myself*…unconditional love. I was asking him to do something that I wasn't even willing to do myself.

The insight was an eye-opener for me. Perhaps the problem didn't lie with my father. Perhaps it lies within my pattern of withholding approval from myself. It was the same lesson that I had been learning as I did my inner child work. I just understood it, for the first time, at a much deeper level.

my father, my teacher

I believe we come to earth with specific goals in mind—soul lessons that we sincerely wish to learn. I also believe it is for this reason that we choose the environment we will come into…the parents we will have, the place we will be born, etc. This doesn't mean that once we incarnate we will always *like* the circumstances we have chosen.

For many years I resented my father for not being the kind of father I wanted. I very much wanted him to be like Jim on the old "Father Knows Best" show. I wanted him to be happy, easy-going, and sensitive. I wanted him to be gentle and call me either "Princess" or "Kitten." Most of all, I wanted to feel cherished by him.

That wasn't the relationship we had. I suspect I was as foreign to my father as he was to me. I'm sure it was especially difficult for him to relate to my sensitive, emotional nature. I was always looking for a deeper level of emotional intimacy with him and I believe that was very threatening to him.

I believe, however, that our relationship—with all of its challenges—had great purpose. It was the perfect vehicle for us to learn the lessons our souls were in need of.

Over the years, I have had more than one trusted "intuitive" tell me that my father and I were in this lifetime together to end a cycle that has run through many lifetimes. "The way your father treated you in this lifetime is the way you treated him in other lifetimes" is how one person explained it.

I have given this much thought. Since I consider this a real possibility, I am committed to doing everything I know how to do to resolve this pattern. I wish this to be the lifetime where the buck stops—where we end this cycle of frustration and hurt.

making progress

I think my father and I have made progress this lifetime. I am very grateful for the three years I spent visiting him weekly. During that time I came to realize that I had never understood my father before.

This relationship has held many lessons for me. I have learned a lot about my father, but I think that I have learned even more about myself. I recently wrote a list of all the lessons I thought my soul was trying to learn through this relationship. The following are some of them:

- I learned that my father really *did* love me.
- I learned that the reason a person is controlling is because they are fearful—and feel so out of control—themselves.
- I learned that our inner children are just as strong in our parents as they are in us.
- I learned the importance of loving myself as unconditionally as possible.
- I learned the steep price I pay when I change who I am in order to win the approval of another.

- I learned that sometimes I have amazing courage.
- I learned that I am committed to my soul's progress.
- And—perhaps the most important lesson of all—I have learned the importance of forgiving both others *and* myself.

wonderful dividends

I have taken many healing steps over the last 20 years, but none have impacted me as greatly as inner child work and the work on my relationship with my father. Now that I have made significant progress in both areas, I have a sense of being almost physically lighter. I feel happier and more playful. I have reaped wonderful rewards for the time and energy I have invested.

It is my most fervent hope that if—in the future—my father and I should once again choose to incarnate together, this time there will be a major difference...this time we will come back as the best of friends. I continue to work toward that goal.

lesson 13

we have to feel in order to heal

Those who do not know how to weep with their whole heart don't know how to laugh either.

Golda Meir

For many years I explored metaphysical and personal growth concepts. I understood the reasoning and logic of many of the new ideas I was considering and consciously worked on implementing them in my life. I enjoyed the intellectual challenge and spiritual exploration. I knew I was making progress in my attitudes; and yet...I didn't really feel significantly better on an emotional level.

Believing that I could rid myself of the pain I felt by talking about it, I spent many, many hours in conversation with trusted friends and relatives exploring past experiences. While it was helpful to intellectually understand what I had been through, it didn't provide me with the relief I was seeking. I still felt like I churned inside—as though at times I contained a cauldron of emotion.

It has taken me many years to understand that I was leaving out a significant part of the healing process—*feeling* the pain. I realize now, as I look back, that I thought I could jump right from the problem to the solution if only I could intellectually understand it.

Unfortunately, healing doesn't work that way. As much as I wanted to avoid walking through the mud of emotional pain, I finally came to the realization that I just plain couldn't avoid it. If I was really going to feel better, then I had to be willing to feel worse first.

the healing that comes from being heard

I used to ask myself why I didn't start working on my relationship with my father years ago. I have come to the conclusion that I wasn't yet ready, nor did I have the skills to do so any sooner. I *wanted* to love my father more deeply; I *wanted* to have a better relationship with him; I just didn't know how to go about it.

Looking back now, I realize that a turning point for me occurred several years ago during a conversation with a dear friend. I told her how emotionally distant my relationship was with my father. I then proceeded to explain the events in his early childhood that I felt had greatly contributed to this situation.

All of a sudden, I had a moment of enlightenment. I realized that my intellectual understanding of why my father was the way he was, and my need to express my emotion regarding his actions, were *two entirely different things*. I recognized that I had never previously allowed myself to really *feel* my pain regarding the relationship—that instead, the minute it would surface, I would try to intellectualize it away. It was the first time I understood that I needed to *acknowledge* the pain I felt.

Soon after, I learned about inner child work and began the process for myself. I found inner child work to be incredibly helpful because it gave me the permission I needed to begin honoring and expressing my feelings. It was an opportunity, for the first time, to acknowledge the little girl within that had felt so angry, so hurt, so rejected. I finally heard her. I wrote down her words, I cried her tears, I expressed her anger.

distancing our feelings

Inner child work was (and still is at times) very challenging for me because I had pushed down so much of the anger and frustration I felt from childhood. As a child I had no idea how to express these emotions in a healthy way. As I got older and experienced the death of my mother and my brother, I added grief, guilt, and depression to the mix.

In my early 20s I still had no idea how to release these feelings so I pushed them down farther and farther by overeating. It was far too threatening to actually feel them. I thought that if I ventured into these feelings I would be totally overwhelmed, so I tried to distance myself from them through food.

I wonder if one of the reasons for this distancing from my emotions was that they didn't make sense intellectually to me. It literally took me years to accept, and express, the anger I felt toward my mother for leaving me when I was 22. The anger didn't seem logical; after all, she hadn't *chosen* to die a painful death from cancer.

I didn't know then that it doesn't matter whether or not something is logical to us. If it hurts, it hurts. Our feelings aren't correct or incorrect…they just *are*. (I have found, however, that after expressing and releasing emotion, I often uncover deep, meaningful reasons for its existence.)

Looking back at my relationship with my father, I suspect I wanted to avoid delving into my feelings because they brought up such guilt. Voicing my deep feelings of hurt, anger, and rejection (even to myself), made me feel like I was a bad daughter.

addressing the pain

I believe another reason why I avoided addressing deep-seated, uncomfortable feelings was because I was afraid that once I brought them out into the open, they would make the situation even worse. It *was* painful to look at the anger and hurt that I had held—much of it since childhood. It was difficult acknowledging all the resentments I had held onto. The process made me feel fearful that the emotions would never diminish in their intensity.

The reality of the situation, however, is that as I gave voice to my feelings—by journaling, by doing inner child exercises, by sharing my feelings with others—I *did* begin to feel better. I began to feel the emotion lessening. Because I had finally *heard* the little child within me, she began to feel safer and more loved.

I have come to understand that a person can't heal without addressing the emotions they carry. A friend of mine once said, "Sometimes you just have to stand still and hurt." I think there is a great deal of wisdom in that statement.

Talking is *not* a substitute for feeling. Neither is eating or drinking or shopping or any other escape mechanism. I consciously try to remember that fact when an issue comes up and my first thought is, "I need ice cream."

I am learning to tell the difference between my physical hunger and an urge to "eat down" my feelings. I am learning to just stand still and hurt. And, as uncomfortable as that is, I am starting to realize that the pain doesn't last forever. Once I feel it, it slowly starts to dissipate. I understand now that the process of feeling our pain causes one sharp blow; the stuffing down of our pain causes a dull ache that lasts forever.

lesson 14

our children are not *our* children

Your children are not your children.
They are the sons and daughters of Life's longing for itself.
They come through you but not from you,
And though they are with you yet they belong not to you.

Kahlil Gibran

When I was in my early 20s I taught elementary school. My first year as a teacher was spent with kindergarteners. I remember some of the beliefs that I held in those days and, in particular, what I held to be true about children. I thought of children as blank slates when they were born; as pieces of putty that parents and society molded. I believed this determined what children would eventually become.

Within about six months of the time I became a parent I threw that belief right out the window. Being around an infant made me realize that they were most definitely *not* blank slates. While children are greatly influenced by their parents and the society in which they grow up, these things are not the only factors which will affect a child's life and experiences. Children are born with distinct personalities and soul lessons to learn.

many levels of awareness

In my early years of parenting I was very aware of my children's differing personalities. I still viewed them at that time as *my* children, though. I felt incredibly responsible—almost too responsible—for them. I was very overprotective and tried to shield both of them from hurts and disappointment. As they grew, though, so did I.

Over the years I have come to expand my beliefs about parenting many times. As Mandy and Matt got older and went to school, I began to realize that it wasn't possible to always shield them from the world— that there were experiences that were out of my control. The older they got, the more I had to learn to let go. For some of us, that doesn't come easily. I had to learn that they had their own lives to live and that often I couldn't shelter them from pain; I could only support them while they went through it.

As I progressed in my own spiritual understanding, I began to view them in a significantly different way. As I started to perceive myself in an expanded way—as a soul incarnating for the purpose of increased awareness—I began to recognize that Mandy and Matthew were here for the same purpose.

I came to understand that they didn't "begin" the day I gave birth to them; they came into existence eons ago. I didn't "create" them during my pregnancy. What I created was their physical bodies. The rest *they* provided. They were souls who came with specific lessons they wanted to work on in this incarnation, just as we all do.

I believe they chose Tom and me as parents because we could provide the experience—for better or for worse—that was optimal for their growth. They aren't *my* children in the sense that I "own" them; they are souls who chose to be born to me.

developing healthy boundaries

Several years ago a friend suggested I read the book *Boundaries—Where You End and I Begin* by Anne Katherine, M.A. It proved to be an incredibly helpful book for me. As I read the concepts, I began to gain more clarity regarding my relationships and my own patterns. Not having grown up with healthy boundaries intact, this was an eye opener.

In her book, Katherine describes boundaries as "a limit or edge that defines you as separate from others." We have physical boundaries, such as our skin, which defines where we leave off and another person begins. We have other types of boundaries as well—emotional, spiritual, sexual, and relational.

Having someone dictate the path you must follow spiritually, for example, would be a violation of your spiritual boundary. Having someone touch you in a way you feel is inappropriate is a violation of your sexual boundary. An attempt by someone to control how you think or feel would be a violation of your emotional boundary.

Our boundaries determine how we will be treated by others. Dr. Phil McGraw contends, "We teach others how to treat us." We do this by what we tolerate or do not tolerate. If we recognize the existence of boundaries, and understand that we are worthy of having healthy boundaries, we will protect ourselves against people and actions that would cross them.

As I worked on strengthening my boundaries, I gained a clearer sense of myself and my relationship to others. The reading of Anne Katherine's book dovetailed beautifully with my own developing understanding of my role with my children. I have come to realize that the development of healthy boundaries is vital to all of our relationships. We have to gain an understanding of "where other people end and we begin" if we hope to honor their path and have them honor ours.

creating healthier relationships

I make it a habit to reread Ms. Katherine's book at least once a year. It seems that each time a different paragraph or idea stands out for me. I have learned a lot about myself in the process.

I have come to recognize that, in the past, I had a pattern of allowing people to say inappropriate things to me—usually, opinions on how I should live my life. I would tolerate these boundary crossings without saying anything. Finally, after repeated violations, I would respond with a great deal of pent-up anger.

Now that I am aware of the existence of boundaries, I work very hard at addressing situations *as* they occur. I now know that I have the right (and responsibility) to protect my boundaries. I work at responding much more appropriately to situations so that I won't have to carry around repressed anger.

Learning that lesson is also helping me in my relationship with my children. I am much more truthful with them about what I am willing to do, or not do, for them. They no longer have to wonder if I am doing something for them while secretly resenting it. There is a much more straightforward dynamic to our relationship now, and that has been a very positive change.

a challenging job

Parenting involves a great deal of hard work. It is much more difficult than I ever dreamt it would be. It has also been much more rewarding than I ever thought it could be. And it has given me a gift I never expected—a much better understanding of myself.

Because of my children I have learned a great deal about my strengths, my weaknesses, and my capacity to love. In wanting life to be better for them, I have made it better for myself. In trying to explain the workings of the world to them, I have had to examine my own beliefs about it. In learning to honor the individuals that they are, I am learning to honor myself also.

My children are now young adults, and I have many dreams for them. I would like to see them healthy and happy. I would like them to develop their talents and choose lifestyles and careers that will bring them fulfillment and balance. But most of all, I would like them to understand that this experience which we call living is a divine and noble adventure which has great purpose, and that their father and I feel deeply blessed to be sharing the journey with them.

lesson 15

it really is...*a Wonderful Life*

I look back upon my youth and realize how so many people gave me help,
understanding, courage—very important things to me—and they never knew it.
They entered into my life and became powers within me. All of us live
spiritually by what others have given us, often unwittingly, in the significant
hours of our life. At the time these significant hours may not even be
perceived. We may not recognize them until years later when we look back, as
one remembers some long-ago music or a boyhood landscape. We all owe to
others much of our gentleness and wisdom that we have made our own; and
we may well ask ourselves what will others owe to us.

Albert Schwietzer

I believe we come into this life with an agenda for our soul's growth. We
choose, on a soul level before we are born, what it is we most need to
learn. In order to accomplish this agenda, we equip ourselves with the
assistance we will need to make that growth possible.

One of the ways in which we do this is by making agreements with
loved ones on a soul level before we are born. We choose to come into
each other's life at a future point so we might have the experiences that
will be most beneficial for our souls.

Some of the agreements we make include friction and difficulty so
that we might learn forgiveness and compassion. At other times, the
arrangement will be much gentler, offering us support and guidance. I

have met up with a number of these supportive companions and they were gifts, coming to me at the moment I needed them most. In their quiet, unassuming ways, they helped change the course of my life.

we touch other lives

I absolutely love the movie *It's a Wonderful Life* with Jimmy Stewart because I believe that it is based in truth; we each have great potential to positively affect the lives of others. And like George Bailey, the character Stewart plays, I would suspect that we really don't know our own impact.

I have been very blessed, and deeply influenced at times, by people who don't even know they touched my life. They include teachers who have expanded my awareness, authors of books that I have benefited greatly from, total strangers who showed me a courtesy.

Sometimes the person did know me well but had no way of knowing how much I had been influenced by them. A former employer of mine, for example, lived her life with such compassion and integrity that she has been a role model to me for over two decades.

Each of these people has influenced my life in their own unique way and I am deeply grateful to them. They have contributed to my becoming more than I would have been had I not met them. Each, in their own way, has contributed to the growth of my soul.

I am especially grateful to family members and friends who have touched my life, for I am aware that these were long-standing agreements we entered into. In addition to offering me love and support, they have often acted as wonderful models for me: my mother's gentleness with others; my friend Susan's ability to deeply nurture a person's body and spirit; the perseverance my daughter and son have in working toward their goals. As I appreciate their gifts and their strengths, it encourages me to work at developing those same qualities in myself.

we give without knowing

There are many small, but significant, memories I hold to my heart. Some of these experiences took place many years ago and oftentimes the person had absolutely no idea they were having an impact upon me. A compliment, a kind gesture, the sharing of a bit of wisdom, the way they lived their life. They are all stored in my memory and in my heart.

At a wedding reception Tom and I attended in our early 20s, a middle-aged man and his wife came up to me. The man said, "My wife and I were talking about what a beautiful complexion you have. We just wanted to tell you." I was highly embarrassed and didn't know what to say. In hindsight, I think about the precious gift this man and his wife gave to me when I was so depressed and in such need of feeling good about myself. How could he possibly have known that I would still treasure his gesture over 25 years later? Such is the impact we have.

You do not have any less influence on others than those that have touched you deeply. You likewise impact others by your attitudes and your actions. Sometimes I think about my mother and how shocked she must have been, once she reached the spirit realm, to find that her death had such a profound impact on so many people. My mother—quiet, gentle, unassuming—couldn't possibly have known that she would be so deeply missed all these years later; that she held such incredible importance to all of us.

being aware of our influence

When we think about the possible influence we have in the lives of others, we come to honor ourselves more deeply. We begin to realize that we *do* make a difference in the world. Our words and our actions *are* important. People *do* notice, whether or not they tell us.

If you are uncertain as to whether or not your life impacts others, consider the impact others have on you. Think back over the last few days. Recall the interactions you have had with your spouse, your children, your co-workers, the checkout person at the supermarket. Ask yourself, "Was I affected by their words or actions?" In all likelihood, you were.

You have every bit of this same potential—for better or for worse. You can be negative and judgmental, causing others to feel badly about themselves, or you can be the brightest spot in their day. You can be the crankiest person that comes through a supermarket cashier's line or you can take the time to recognize that this is another precious soul, just like you, and smile at him or her.

It's all up to you. It's your choice. And at the end of the day when you are quiet with yourself, you will more easily answer the question, "Is the world a better place—a bit kinder, a bit more compassionate— because I walked here this day?"

lesson 16

we can find guidance in the words of others

If I can stop one heart from breaking,
I shall not live in vain;
If I can ease one life the aching,
Or cool one pain,
Or help one fainting robin
Unto his nest again,
I shall not live in vain.

Emily Dickinson

I first read this poem in December of 1972 in a copy of *Family Circle* magazine. I was instantly moved as I read the words. They spoke to me on a deep level. These words have become my creed. For many years I kept this poem tucked away in a drawer where I periodically took it out and read it.

When we furnished our home office, I wanted the room to be a very spiritual space and wanted to surround myself with items that held particular significance to me. This poem now sits on my bookshelf, enclosed in a lovely floral print frame, inspiring me as it has for over 30 years.

there is inspiration all around us

Over the years, I have been immensely blessed by words; words that came in the form of quotations, poems, short stories, and affirmations. Often they have held deep meaning for me.

I particularly appreciate quotations. I use a daily planner and keep a special section in it to write down the quotations that I want to remember. I take my planner with me much of the time and when I am in a situation where I have a few "extra" minutes—in a doctor's waiting room, in a restaurant waiting for a friend to arrive, in a coffee shop where I am pampering myself—I enjoy rereading some of my favorite quotes.

Sometimes these words bring me humor—a laugh when I most need it. Sometimes they bring me a wonderful, warm feeling that I am connected with another human being by a shared vision of the world. Sometimes (often, in fact) they bring me new insights; new ways of viewing the world.

I am most grateful for quotations that bring me the gift of guidance. It is as though I have a grand collection of men and women, far wiser than I will probably ever be, supporting me as I walk upon the earth. Lessons they have learned (I'm sure oftentimes with much difficulty and persistence), they pass on to me so my path will be smoother.

Because of the insights I have received, I have been spared some of the mistakes I'm sure I would have otherwise made. The quotations have taught me wonderful perspectives on compassion and courage and growth. Through them I have seen a grander vision of what mankind can choose to become. If I am open to it, their wisdom can become mine.

the value to others

Both my daughter and my son share my love of quotations. My son collects his favorites in a book that he uses just for this purpose. He especially appreciates quotes that appeal to his sense of humor.

My daughter uses quotations as a means of understanding and expressing herself. She has a favorite gift she received called *A Box of Thoughts on Solitude* that contains slips of paper with short quotes on solitude. She said she finds meaning in reading them for two reasons: first, it gives her comfort to know that others feel the same way she does, and second, they are able to express what she is feeling when she may not be able to. (She says it is a "Yes—that's it!" moment.)

Mandy also has a "wall of sayings" in her apartment. She has chosen statements that represent what she believes and who she is, and has framed them. She only includes those that she resonates with 100%. She has found that it is a way for her to express her own personality.

a multitude of sources

The opportunities for finding meaningful quotations, affirmations, and other writings are almost endless. Louise Hay has wonderful collections of self-empowering affirmations. Sarah Ban Breathnach's work includes quotations designed to bring you a greater sense of self and the abundance that surrounds you. The current *Chicken Soup for the Soul* series of books has brought together hundreds of short stories designed to inspire and enlighten.

Some of my favorite quotations come from Albert Schweitzer, Anaïs Nin, and Kahlil Gibran, but there are many dozens of others who have also contributed to my life. Bookstores are a veritable playground for those of us who seek to expand ourselves in this way.

If it is your desire to benefit from the wisdom of others, ask Spirit to bring to you what would be for your greatest good. Rest assured it will find its way to you!

lesson 17

the most effective prayer is "thank you"

If the only prayer you ever say in your entire life is thank you, it will be enough.

Meister Eckhart

For most of my life I subscribed to the "begging" method in my relationship with God. When I truly desired something, I would implore and plead. "Please help me. Please help me. Please help me." I assumed the role of a powerless child begging her parent. Perhaps I thought I could wear God down until He said, "Enough already! I'll do what you want!"

I realize now that, in begging, I was actually making it harder for myself to achieve my goal. What I was doing was reinforcing in my own mind the distance between where I was and where I wanted to be (or what I wanted to have). I was adding more and more energy to a belief of lack—to the fear that I wasn't really going to get it.

As time has gone on, I have worked at making a shift in the way I view my relationship with God. (Something that has taken a great deal of conscious effort.) As I started releasing the belief that God was a God of judgment and harshness, I began to view our relationship as much more loving and amiable.

The more I came to recognize how profoundly *I* impacted my life by my beliefs and attitudes, the less I felt like God was doing things *to* me. I started to realize that God wasn't the enemy; that God was my partner.

a more effective approach

I take a different approach now in manifesting my heart's desires and find it to be much more effective. When I want to bring something into my life, I communicate this to God and approach it as though it has already come about. Instead of begging, "Please, please…" I thank God. "Thank you for _____. I trust that if this is for my highest good, and the highest good of all, that it will come into being."

When I say "thank you," the energy I am putting forth is one of trust and assurance that I am working in conjunction *with* God. It is a much more positive energy.

If the issue I am praying about is a troubling one, after I speak with God in this manner, I try not to worry about the situation. (I know—easier said than done!) I do my very best to turn it over to God.

seeking God's help

I once heard this "turning a situation over to God" process likened to a child buying a candy bar at a store. If the child offers the clerk a dollar in payment but then, at the last moment, pulls it back, the storekeeper cannot give him the candy.

I try to remember this image when I am tempted to worry about a problem that I have already sought God's help on. I create a picture in my mind of turning over the dollar bill (the problem) to God. I then let it go and trust (as best I can) that my prayer was heard and all will be well.

For situations that are of particular concern to me, I may have to repeat the "turning over" process again and again for an extended period of time. Whenever I start to become fearful about the situation, I try to catch my thoughts as quickly as I can and see the image of turning the problem back over to God.

I have found that this process becomes easier with practice. I have come to the conclusion that it is a much more effective way to pray than what I used to do. Through this "turning over" process, I have seen situations work out when I thought there could be no solution. Each time that happens, it makes it a bit easier for me to turn the next concern over to God while saying, "thank you."

lesson 18

happiness is in the present moment

Life is made of small pleasures. Good eye contact over the breakfast table with your wife. A moment of touching with a friend. Happiness is made of those tiny successes. The big ones come too infrequently. If you don't have all of those zillions of tiny successes, the big ones don't mean anything. If there is one thing I want my children to learn from me, it is to take pleasure in life's daily small successes. It is the most important thing I've learned.

Norman Lear

When my daughter was just a few months old she was prone to running high temperatures and becoming suddenly ill. I often thought how nice it would be when she could talk so that she could tell me exactly where it hurt or how she felt. She began to speak at a young age, and I was thrilled. What I hadn't anticipated was that there would be times when I would long for silence in the years to come—that I would become impatient with listening to a toddler's constant chatter and tired of answering the question, "Why?" numerous times each day.

Before my daughter went to kindergarten, I longed for the time when I would have a few cherished hours to myself each day. After I walked Mandy to the bus on the first day of school and watched this tiny little person walk up those big steps, I went into the house and cried. I knew in that moment that our lives would never be the same—that I could no longer protect and shelter her as I had. I had gotten the freedom that I wanted, but I hadn't foreseen the cost.

I learned a valuable lesson from my daughter's childhood—don't wish the present away. Yes, the next stage would have wonderful benefits. But it would also have difficulties that I hadn't foreseen. I came to the conclusion that each stage of life has its gifts *and* its challenges, and I no longer wanted to wish any of it away. It was precious just as it was.

I am deeply grateful to Mandy for teaching me this lesson. In the last few years I have come to an even deeper understanding of its meaning. I am working at incorporating an awareness and appreciation of the present moment into my everyday attitudes.

staying in the present

It has taken me many years to realize that I used to spend very little time mentally in the present. I spent much of my time thinking about how good things were going to be "when"…(when we got a new house/when I lost weight/when the baby slept through the night, etc.) The list was endless. *That* was when I was finally going to be happy.

When I turned 40 I suddenly thought, "Wait a minute. When am I going to start enjoying this trip?" It was becoming evident to me that I would never have the thin, lithe body that I so envied; that even if I got the newer house there could still be things I didn't like about it; that the crying baby who kept me awake at night would probably, in the future, be keeping me awake praying that she/he would drive safely. It finally occurred to me that things never do get perfect. That was a real awakening for me.

I have so much more enjoyment in my life now that I experience it as it unfolds. I consciously bring my awareness to the present moment as much as possible. The amazing thing is that I have found I have a much better life than I thought I did!

There were so many rich little moments that I didn't appreciate fully before. There are priceless, precious moments each day just waiting for my awareness...listening to my children laugh at a shared joke, having my husband compliment me on a good dinner, noticing the lovely shade of green that the leaves possess in the spring. This is where the real wealth in my life lies. It is in all of the dozens of tiny moments that occur each day.

lesson 19

perfectionism is a double-edged sword

Perfectionism is self-abuse of the highest order.

Anne Wilson Schaef

When I was in the seventh grade, I was already very close to my oldest brother, Norm (who by then was in the seminary studying to be a Catholic priest). We regularly exchanged long letters. That December he came home for Christmas and we had an opportunity to stay up late and talk. As we sat looking at the sparkling lights of the Christmas tree we discussed a number of different topics.

I clearly recall one of the topics being the letters we exchanged. I told him that the reason it took me so long to write was that I would often recopy the letters several times to make sure they didn't contain spelling errors. Norm looked at me in great surprise and said, "Don't you know that I don't care about the spelling? I just love hearing from you. It's okay to make mistakes."

I still remember that conversation even though it took place so very many years ago. It was an eye opener for me. The truth was, I *didn't* know it was okay to make mistakes. I thought I had to be perfect in order to be accepted. I *didn't* know that I was good enough just the way I was.

Perfectionism is a double-edged sword. While some might argue that it leads us to do our very best, I would suggest that it doesn't benevolently motivate us; it drives us out of fear. It drains the pleasure out of experiences and robs us of the opportunity to take pride in our work. It keeps us perpetually searching for the Holy Grail—a mythical "perfect" way of doing things.

Perfectionism expressed itself in my life through a persistent feeling of not having accomplished enough, no matter how much I did. It gave me a feeling of futility about not having done things exactly right, not having done them perfectly. It didn't matter to me if someone else thought that I had done an excellent job on a project; I always knew, in hindsight, that it would have been even better if only I had done it a different way.

Now that I am more aware of the dynamics of my own inner dialogues, I recognize perfectionism for what it is—the voice of my inner critical parent haranguing me.

stopping ourselves before we begin

I now see that my pattern of perfectionism has prevented me, on many occasions, from taking on new experiences. Because I was so afraid that I wouldn't be able to do a task perfectly, I chose not to do it at all. It was a way of protecting myself, of not subjecting myself to the harsh words of my inner critical parent: "You probably wouldn't have done very well at that. What made you think you could do it, anyway? You're really not as capable as other people."

I wonder how different my life would have been had I not been encumbered with the issue of perfectionism. I wonder how many things I would have tried only to find, even if I couldn't do them incredibly well, I would still have enjoyed them immensely. Changing the pattern of perfectionism within myself is one of my constant challenges.

insight from Spirit

Several years ago I took a very positive step toward releasing the pattern when I accepted the position of director of our local volunteer center. It was a very demanding job and entailed a great number of responsibilities that I had not previously undertaken: speaking in public, being interviewed by newspapers, holding committee meetings, organizing large community events. I felt very fearful because of my inexperience. I found my perfectionism coming forward very strongly. I asked Spirit frequently for guidance and was led to the following quote:

Anything worth doing is worth doing poorly, until you can learn to do it well.

Steve Brown

I read that quote each morning as I sat at my desk. It helped allay the fears I felt about doing the day's tasks perfectly. It reminded me that I just had to do the best job I could and that, as I became more experienced, I would do the job better.

taking steps toward change

Despite all the work I have done on myself, I have found that the pattern of perfectionism still creeps into my life. While it usually brings with it great discomfort, I am making progress seeing it for what it is: a pattern I am working on releasing. That helps me to loosen its stronghold. I purposefully engage my inner nurturing parent and speak lovingly to the child within myself. "You *are* good enough. You don't have to be perfect for me to accept you. I love you just as you are."

I have found that to judge myself harshly for the continued presence of this pattern would be to reinforce it. "You aren't over this entirely? See, you really aren't good enough." Instead, I find it most effective to treat myself gently. "Oh, that is a thought about needing to be perfect. I choose not to believe that anymore. I don't have to be perfect to be accepted by myself or others. I love myself the way I am."

And now, when I am writing a note to a friend and misspell a word, I purposefully cross it out and write over top the correct spelling. I don't rewrite the entire note. It is then I smile inside because I know that I am making progress.

lesson 20

we are capable of facing fear

We CANNOT escape fear. We can only transform it into a companion that accompanies us on all our exciting adventures...

Susan Jeffers

Fear has many faces and enters into our lives in many different ways. Overcoming fear seems to be a very significant challenge in my life. As a child I was often fearful. I worried a great deal. My family teased me about being a "worrywart." As an adult, I am learning to take steps to face the situations that cause me to feel such anxiety.

I became motivated to work on my fear issues once I began to understand the power that we have to create our lives. I started to realize that by constantly replaying a fear over and over again in my mind, I was actually adding energy to it and increasing the likelihood of its being realized. Since this was not what I wanted in my life, I began to work on identifying and dealing with my fears.

the duality of fear

At times, fear serves an incredibly important purpose in our life—to keep us safe and protected. It can act as an internal warning signal telling us that we need to take action in order to safeguard our physical body. After traveling on a patch of ice-covered roadway, for instance, the presence of fear motivates us to reduce our speed and drive more cautiously.

This type of fear is very constructive and can literally save our life. A second type of fear—"destructive"—can do just the opposite. Instead of adding to the quality of our life, it diminishes it. Instead of protecting us and spurring us on to positive action, it can cause us to become caught in a cycle of worry and inaction.

Destructive fear manifests uniquely in each person's life. It may include a fear of failure, fear of rejection, fear of illness or injury, fear of not having enough money. There are numerous ways in which it surfaces in each of us. The end result, however, is often the same…it is a negative, paralyzing, time-consuming, and energy-draining force.

The challenge we are faced with lies in discerning the difference between fear that is constructive (and safeguards us physically) and fear that is destructive (and leads to a perpetual feeling of anxiety.)

at our most vulnerable

I have come to realize that the time when I am most vulnerable to destructive fear is at night. I will settle in to bed, ready for sleep, and fearful thoughts will creep up on me. My mind skips from situation to situation. Before I know it, an hour has passed and I am *wide* awake. I have learned, through experience, that the middle of the night is *not* the time for me to be examining issues. Fatigue prevents me from being objective and thinking clearly.

The most effective way for me to deal with these night-time "worry fests" is to get out of bed and write down my concerns. *Everything* that I am fretting about gets listed on a piece of paper. I do this with a solemn promise to myself that I will deal with the problems in the morning.

I have found that I am much more effective in dealing with issues when I am rested. I am often amazed, when I read over the note from the previous night, at just how dramatic and life-threatening everything looks at 3:00 am. Because of this, I try to avoid entering into these nighttime episodes of anxiety.

addressing the fear

It is vitally important for each of us to develop coping skills to deal with the fear that surfaces in our life. If we don't, we will retard our spiritual, emotional, and mental growth and prevent ourselves from experiencing fulfilling, satisfying lives.

I have found the following approaches to be very valuable in helping me release fear:

• Differentiate the fear
• Become grounded in the present
• Ask for spiritual guidance
• Chart a plan of action
• Seek an understanding of the "big picture"
• Take the action you fear
• Recognize the challenge of success

The following sections will explain these approaches in more detail.

1. differentiating our fears

Fear is part of the human experience. I have yet to meet anyone who hasn't grappled with it. I have, however, met people who were masters at dealing with it. One of them, Carl Franklin, a spiritual teacher, spoke with me about the importance of examining our fears so that we could understand them and effectively respond to them.

Carl made the following suggestion to me: "In a situation where you feel fearful, stop and ask yourself if you are *really* in imminent danger. If you are, take the necessary steps to make yourself safe. If you are not in immediate danger, you are playing 'What if.' In that case, *you* are creating the fear and have the power to change it."

I try to remember Carl's words when I am faced with a situation where I feel anxious. I ask myself, "Am I in real danger or is my imagination conjuring up 'What if...' scenarios?" (What if I don't get the job? What if one of my loved ones gets ill? What if I'm not able to solve the problem I am facing?)

If I am in *actual* danger (which I find rarely happens), I take the appropriate steps to protect myself. If the danger exists in my imagination, which is much more likely, becoming objective helps me to consciously choose alternate thoughts.

2. becoming grounded in the present

I have found that one of the most effective means for me to deal with destructive fear is to get firmly grounded in the present. I work at recognizing that, in most situations, my fear stems from leaving the present and stepping into the future. (A friend of mine likens this to worrying about labor and delivery when you first find out you are pregnant. By the time you are nine months pregnant, feel huge, and have swollen ankles, you may be more than ready to have the baby be born regardless of how much it may hurt.)

When I am back in the present moment, I concentrate on just being in my body—feeling my feet on the floor and being conscious of whether I am standing or sitting. I then take three deep breaths to get centered. I ask myself if I am safe here and now. More often than not I realize that at this moment I *am* safe, but have been terrorizing myself with thoughts of "What if?"

3. ask for spiritual guidance

I believe *the very most important thing we can do* when confronting a fearful thought is to ask for spiritual guidance. The following prayer is one that I learned several years ago. It is a prayer I say on a regular basis:

Holy Spirit, help me to experience this the way You would. Remove
me/elevate me/move me through this. Let me perceive this situation
as You would.

I have found it to be incredibly helpful, whenever I am feeling
fearful, to ask for the assistance of Spirit in dealing with the issue. By
saying this prayer, I am requesting not only guidance and assistance, but
a larger perspective of the issue as well.

Sometimes I need to remind myself of the power of God when I am
asking for His assistance. At those times I picture the Grand Canyon in
my mind—in all of its breathtaking splendor—and say to myself, "God
created the Grand Canyon. What makes me think He doesn't have the
power to help me with this situation?" Sometimes we just need to be
reminded that we don't walk this path alone.

4. chart a plan of action

As we examine our fears more closely, we come to realize that some of
them contain very legitimate concerns. They point out an area of our life
(our health, our finances, a relationship, etc.) that needs focused
attention. We have the choice of either facing the issue and deciding a
course of action, or denying the problem and trying to ignore the fear.
(Which obviously doesn't work, but we all still try it!)

I have been faced with several of these unsettling fears in the past
year. One of them regarded an aspect of my physical health. I have been
blessed with good health for most of my life, so it was very disturbing
to me when I started to experience recurring pain. I sought medical
attention and started to realize that there were a number of changes I
needed to make in my lifestyle if I wanted to improve the situation.

I felt overwhelmed at the prospect of needing to change so many
things. It brought up great fear in me. I knew I needed to face the

situation, though, so I set about trying to make it more manageable for myself.

I decided that I would implement the changes over a one-year period. I bought a folder, entitled it *52 Steps to More Healthful Living*, and set about making one change each week. Once I had a plan of action I found that my fear level gradually lessened. I began making the changes that had so overwhelmed me initially.

This experience has been a wonderful reminder to me of the strength we have to tackle an intimidating challenge. The solution lies in facing the dilemma head-on and breaking it down into smaller, more manageable pieces. What we *can't* do all at once, we often *can* do in smaller steps. Instead of using our energy to cope with fear, we channel our energy into action so that the fear can be released.

5. seek an understanding of the "big picture"

Probably the most meaningful step I have taken to reduce my personal fear level has been to gain a clearer understanding of the "big picture" spiritually. When my mother and brother died, I was devastated because I didn't really know if they existed any longer. I have spent a great deal of time over the past 25 years exploring answers about the nature of reality. I have come to understand that we truly don't die…only our body does. Our spirit—our essence—goes on forever. This knowledge has helped me immensely.

These insights were a source of much comfort for me during the last two weeks of my father's illness. I didn't feel, as I had with my mother and brother, a gut-wrenching sense of fear for his well-being once he passed. I understood that the process is one of benevolence and love.

Several times each day, at both the hospital and the hospice home, I would go off by myself (usually to a bathroom, the only place of privacy). I would take a few moments to turn my attention and thoughts inward. Each time I could sense the calming words, "All is well. All is well. It may not look like it, but all is well."

Those meaningful words were a wonderful reminder to me of the "big picture." My father *was* safe. He was just preparing to leave his body and live as pure spirit. The knowledge of this process didn't prevent me from feeling that my heart was breaking each time I looked at him. What it did prevent me from feeling was *fear*.

6. take the action you fear

I used to think that I was defective because I experienced so much fear in my life. I looked at the progress others made in their lives and assumed that they were accomplishing these feats totally unencumbered by fear. I believed I was somehow innately inferior to them because of this.

I have come to realize that my fear was not a sign of being defective; it was a case of misunderstanding reality. I had always interpreted fear as an indication that I should stop whatever it was I was contemplating...applying for a different job, taking on a challenging task, being more honest in a relationship. The list was endless.

I gave a tremendous amount of power to fear. I didn't know that *everyone* feels fear...not just me. I also didn't know that the presence of fear did not mean that I shouldn't attempt a task. (I am, of course, not promoting putting yourself in any situation where you would be in physical danger.) I am suggesting that you examine your beliefs about fear.

One of the most fearful challenges I have ever undertaken was the writing of this book. Initially, it was the process of writing itself that threatened me. ("What makes me think I can write a book? I'm not a writer!") As I became more comfortable with the process of writing, the fears that dominated were about being so emotionally naked and vulnerable.

In order to proceed with the book, I had to keep a notebook next to me. In it I wrote all the fears that surfaced. I filled up page after page with my fears.

Of great assistance to me during this time was a book by Susan Jeffers, Ph.D., entitled *Feel The Fear And Do It Anyway*. I found this book immensely helpful because it assisted me in releasing the inaccurate belief that I was the only one who experienced fear. It helped me to understand that *everyone experiences fear* and that it can be overcome.

I am extremely thankful that I didn't allow my fears to keep me from the writing of this book. It has been a life-changing experience for me. I see, in hindsight, that it was the next step on my own healing journey.

7. recognize the challenge of success

Sometimes fear is present in very surprising ways. Several years ago, when I was grappling with whether or not to make a career move, a friend said to me, "Has it occurred to you that maybe what you fear is not failure, but success?" My first reaction was that she was incorrect. Why would I be *afraid* of success?

I did take her words to heart, though, and started paying attention to the anxiety that arose when I considered moving into the new field of work. Soon enough I began to realize that her words were, in fact, accurate…there were times when I was very fearful of succeeding. This came as a complete surprise to me.

As I thought, and journaled, about the fears that surfaced regarding changes I was considering, I was reminded of a quotation I had read by Marianne Williamson. I have read and reread these words many times since then. I believe that they hold profound truth. Like me, you may have read Marianne's quote many times before, but I believe that each time we read it we have the opportunity to relate to it on a deeper level.

Our deepest fear

is not that we are inadequate.

Our deepest fear

is that we are powerful beyond measure.

It is our light, not our darkness that frightens

us most.

We ask ourselves,

who am I to be brilliant, gorgeous, talented,

fabulous?

Actually, who are you not to be?

You are a child of God.

Your playing small doesn't serve the world.

There's nothing enlightened about shrinking

so that other people won't feel insecure

around you.

We were born to make manifest the glory of

God within us.

It is not just in some of us; it's in everyone.

And, as we let our own light shine, we

unconsciously give other people permission

to do the same.

As we are liberated from our own fear,

our presence automatically liberates others.

When I find myself feeling anxious about possible success, I take out the above quotation and read it again and again until I feel calmer. It reminds me of my connectedness with God and that I have a divine purpose in the world. It also reminds me that I need to rise above my inclination to "play small." It gives me the courage to take my next step.

understanding our patterns

I am always amazed at how visceral my fears are, and how childlike and helpless I initially feel about them. I am coming to understand that the reason for this is because many of these fears are the same fears I experienced as a child; they are just cloaked in adult circumstances now.

As I work to gain insights into my patterns of fear, I am beginning to see their repetitive nature. I am beginning to identify particular fears that surface over and over (fears of not being good enough, of not being accepted, etc.). It has been beneficial for me to become more objective about my fears so that when they present themselves once again, I am better equipped to recognize them. The objectivity reminds me that these core fear issues are "workbook pages" on lessons that my soul wants to learn.

viewing it differently

I used to feel incredibly ashamed of being fearful. I thought it meant I was weak. I now realize that we all experience fear. It oftentimes just shows us what we perceive to be our limitations. The older I get, the more I challenge those limits. Frequently, in hindsight, I will think, "Now what made me think I *couldn't* do that?"

I am beginning to realize that fear has only the power *I* give to it; that many—if not most—of my limitations are self-imposed; that I have much more potential than I ever realized. And, along the way, I am learning that we aren't courageous because we lack a sense of fear; we are courageous because we move forward in spite of it.

part 3

healing activities

Autobiography in five short chapters

A poem by Portia Nelson

Chapter one

I walk down the street.

    There is a deep hole in the sidewalk.

    I fall in.

    I am lost...I am helpless.

        It isn't my fault.

It takes forever to find a way out.

Chapter two

I walk down the same street.

    There is a deep hole in the sidewalk.

    I pretend I don't see it.

    I fall in again.

I can't believe I am in this same place.

        But, it isn't my fault.

It still takes a long time to get out.

Chapter three

I walk down the same street.

    There is a deep hole in the sidewalk.

    I *see* it is there.

    I still fall in...it's a habit...but,

        my eyes are open.

        I know where I am.

It is *my* fault.

I get out immediately.

Chapter four

I walk down the same street.

    There is a deep hole in the sidewalk.

    I walk around it.

Chapter five

I walk down another street.

healing activities

In my experience, each person's healing path is uniquely his or her own. The best way to discover the direction most beneficial for you is to ask the guidance of Spirit. Ask, and then trust that you will be guided, for you will.

As I have progressed and had more and more experiences of being led to the right person, course, book, healing method, etc., it has become much easier for me to trust that Spirit will guide me toward healing. I never cease to be amazed, in hindsight, at how many times I find "just the right book" in the midst of a complete stack or will speak to "just the right person" to hear what I need to hear that day. The ways of Spirit are nothing short of miraculous if we open our awareness to them.

I have been guided to take many steps on my journey toward healing. Some of the steps I have taken have been particularly helpful. They have enabled me to better understand both myself and my relationship to God. I share these activities with you now in hopes that they may assist you in your growth also.

activity 1

set your course consciously

Several years ago I was privileged to attend a Franklin Quest™ training seminar that explained the concept behind the use of the company's planners. I found the seminar to be extremely beneficial. In it, the speaker took us through a process that enabled us to look at our lives from a larger perspective, identifying those things that were truly important to us. I have thought back to this seminar many times and been grateful for the experience of attending it. Because of it, I started to consciously think about my priorities and the direction I wanted to set for my life.

It is incredibly easy to get so caught up with the everyday tasks and responsibilities of life that we lose a larger perspective. What is it we *really* hold important in our lives? What do we want to accomplish? Are we living our life in accordance with these priorities? Have we even taken the time to discover them to begin with?

As we begin to define our priorities, it is as though we are developing a map for our lives. This map reminds us of our destination and, in the event we get off course, can help us to reestablish our direction. It offers landmarks (experiences) to let us know if we are going the right way. And, because it shows us our destination, we will know when we have arrived.

I would highly recommend that you take the necessary time to establish *your* priorities and the goals you have for your life. Spend some quiet time thinking about what is *really* important to you. Engage a friend in the process if you feel that would be helpful. (When Tom was developing his list, and I was refining mine, we had a number of conversations that helped both of us gain more clarity.) Once you have recognized those things that hold the greatest importance for you, you will be able to clearly ask yourself, "Am I living my life *now* in ways that reflect my highest priorities?"

activity 2

begin to listen

I used to do a lot more talking *at* Tom than I did talking *with* him. After being married for a few years I began to resent what I perceived to be his lack of communication with me. Several years ago, my daughter and I had a conversation in which she aired her frustrations with my not listening to her. I was truly shocked. I thought I *had* been listening!

It occurred to me that maybe the reason Tom didn't talk more was because I didn't listen enough. I am making a concerted effort now with all of my family members to really listen to them more deeply. I am learning that, at times, the very best thing I can do to encourage communication is to simply be with them and be still; to give them time to formulate their thoughts and arrange their words.

I suspect this is a lot like our relationship with Spirit. We just can't hear if we don't truly take the time to listen. If what we want is guidance and help and insight, it doesn't serve us well to bombard God with prayers and then get up and walk away right when He starts to answer us.

Our society values action. It values speed. Ask the average person how they have been lately and they will answer, "I have been so busy!" While modern-day technology has been a blessing to us in many ways, it has also created a very impatient society. We want answers and we want them now. I have found that there is a direct correlation between my busyness and my ability to listen to Spirit. When I am frenzied, stressed, and tired, it is very difficult for me to listen. When I am calmer and more grounded, it is much easier.

It takes a conscious choice to temporarily step off the treadmill and detach from an agitated frame of mind; to take a deep breath and calm ourselves down. It takes awareness for us to take time out from our *doing* to just *be*. Whatever process a person uses—meditation, spending quiet time out in nature, soaking in a warm bath while listening to soothing music, etc.—it is vital to find a place of centeredness within ourselves. It enables us to listen. It opens us up to being receptive to the guidance of Spirit.

It is important to take time each day to be peaceful. One of the ways in which I do this is to start my day with a few minutes of prayer and meditation. It sets the tone (and my intentions) for the day. It also gives me an opportunity to ask God to be present in all my activities of the day. I once read that starting your day without prayer is like playing an instrument in a concert without taking the time to tune the instrument. My experience has proven this to be true.

Time spent in centeredness need not be formal or even long. It could be five minutes of finding a quiet space, getting comfortable, and consciously relaxing your body. It is a time to turn inward and be in silence. Prayer is our *talking* to God; relaxation, meditation, and quiet times are our opportunities to *listen*.

activity 3

take time to journal

As I mentioned previously, I have kept journals periodically throughout my lifetime. I wrote according to my need. I didn't use them as diaries to record everyday events; I used them to record feelings and thoughts, joys and frustrations. The more confused I was, the longer the entry became.

I found that journaling made me feel better. It helped me to release my feelings and to feel emotionally lighter. Once I had released some of the emotion attached to a situation, it was a bit easier for me to gain the objectivity I needed to work on the issue.

Several years ago I decided to begin journaling with more frequency as a way of understanding aspects of myself that still confused me. The experience turned out to be incredibly revealing.

As I looked back over the journals I had kept previously, I realized how very difficult it had been for me to write the truth about how I felt. I had often prefaced entries with an apology: "I hope I am not going to look at this journal entry ten years from now and judge it harshly," or "I feel so embarrassed about writing today. I feel like I should know how to handle this." It started occurring to me just how difficult it was for me to be truly honest (even with myself) without fear of judgment.

I began to realize that if I was going to benefit fully from journaling, I needed to be able to express myself in an open, no-holds-barred fashion. I made a pact with myself that I would write as truthfully as possible. In exchange, I would refrain from any self-criticism about the contents.

In the past few years I have done a great deal of writing in my journals. Now that I write on a more consistent basis, I am finding that I am becoming increasingly comfortable with writing down my true feelings—no matter what they are.

If I am feeling judgmental of myself before I write, I will print in large bold letters at the top of the page a reminder to myself: "NO JUDGMENT—ONLY HONESTY." It reminds me that the purpose of the process is to gain clarity, and I will only achieve that by suspending judgment about myself and being honest with my feelings. An attitude of self-criticism only discourages me from fully expressing my feelings.

the issue of privacy

One of the issues that often comes up for people when they think about starting a journal is the issue of privacy. It is important that you maintain the amount of security that you need to feel safe with your writing. (After all, the goal in writing is to express the *real* you—not the airbrushed image that we so often show the world.)

For a particularly sensitive topic, you may decide to destroy the journal entry once you have finished it. (The overriding value of journaling lies in the *process* of expressing our thoughts and emotion.) I have found it helpful, on occasion, to actually burn the piece of paper in a symbolic gesture of turning the situation over to Spirit.

If you choose to keep your writing, there are a variety of options for safeguarding it. Could you keep your journal in a special drawer that the rest of the family doesn't go into? Could you enter your writing into your computer and protect it with a password? Do you have a space in your home (no matter how small) that is yours exclusively? Could you purchase an inexpensive metal box that locks?

If you find yourself saying that there isn't *any* way you could find a safe spot for your writings, you may want to consider the possibility that security isn't the issue. Perhaps the real issue is that you are frightened to delve so truthfully into yourself.

getting started

I usually do my journaling in my home office with the door closed, curled up in the security of my wing-back chair. I have a white candle on an end table next to the chair. I light the candle before I begin, to remind myself that what I am doing is soul work and deserves respect. I take a moment to ask for divine guidance. I ask the writing angels to assist me in the process and to give me clarity with the issue I am writing about.

I usually don't use a fancy book for journaling, but you can use whatever book best suits you. (There are a large variety of books available in stationery stores, bookstores, gift shops, and even grocery stores.) I use spiral bound, lined notebooks that can be purchased just about anywhere. I enjoy getting them from the bookstores of the colleges my children attend. It makes them special to me.

The reason I avoid pretty journals is because oftentimes this isn't "pretty" work. I want my entries to be as accurate as I can make them, and I am more comfortable expressing strong emotions in a plain notebook.

I typically write at night when it is quiet and my family is asleep. That is by no means the only way, or time, to do it. It can be done at any time or in any situation where you seek clarity or feel the need to express yourself.

I have journaled in a variety of places and under a number of different circumstances. I have written in a doctor's waiting room to lessen the anxiety I felt over an impending test result. I have written while looking out at a lake to express the deep joy I felt at that moment. I have written in the car while waiting to bring my son home from a baseball practice. In fact, I have gotten into the habit of keeping paper readily available so that I can express my thoughts whenever I might feel the need to write.

the content

There is no right or wrong way to journal. There are no hard and fast guidelines as to the frequency, the content, the length. It is whatever *you* want it to be; whatever suits your needs. To aid the process, however, I would recommend setting honesty as a priority, and being as gentle with yourself as you can possibly be.

Journaling is soul work. Through this process we dare to take a look at our "dragons"—those areas of ourselves that we are afraid to visit. Often, we are not sure what lies in the inner recesses of our thoughts and emotions. I believe the fear that arises from facing our dragons is that we will discover there is something so horrible about us that if it were to be brought into the light, people would take their love away. After all, we reason, if there is something about us that even *we* aren't willing to view, how would someone else come to accept it?

I have found that journaling is a safe way for me to explore these dragons. It is frequently not easy looking at them, and at times I can feel a great deal of anxiety about doing so. The process sometimes requires all the courage I can muster.

Once I acknowledge a facet of myself that is less than charming, however, it becomes a bit less frightening to me. As I explore my anger, frustration, and hurt, I often come to realize that these feelings are covering up a deeper layer of fear: fear of not being good enough; fear of being abandoned; fear of being unlovable. Where once I thought lay a dragon, now instead stands a little child in pain. Once I have the courage to really listen to that child, I take a step toward healing her.

the benefits

I have found that the more I journal, the more I benefit from it. For many years I journaled sporadically. Now that it has become an integral part of my growth, I would miss it deeply if I weren't able to do it. It is a gift I give myself. It is one of the ways in which I invest in myself. It contributes to my mental health and my relationships with both others and myself.

I see a change in myself now that I have been writing on a more regular basis. For one thing, I miss it if I go too long without journaling. I miss the process of getting in touch with myself in this way. It is as though I need to touch base with an old friend.

It is also much easier for me to get straight to the point in my entries now and not feel that I have to apologize when I am out-of-sorts. It is helping me to gain a much deeper understanding of who I am and what I struggle with. It is also helping me to accept myself in my entirety. In short, the process is helping me to be kinder and gentler to myself.

spiritual assistance through writing

I find that journaling is one of the methods Spirit uses to speak to me. Spirit often gives me insights as I write, and I am very grateful for this help. Sometimes I experience the assistance as a newfound objectivity about a personal issue. After journaling I will find that, instead of being caught up in the issue, I can view it with a much clearer perspective. Often I am able to better understand what it is that I am *really* upset about.

Sometimes, through journaling, I will gain insights into someone else. After I write about my frustration with another person's actions, I will feel more grounded. Releasing my emotion regarding the situation allows me to view it more objectively and begin to understand the other person's position. Oftentimes this process will help me identify the deeper issues that were at play for both of us.

On more than one occasion I have tapped into what I believe are memories from a past life. When this occurs, I try to just let the experience flow and not judge it or be critical of myself. Instead of saying, "This is stupid; I bet I'm making this up," I have learned to just let the words flow. I have had more than one deeply healing insight come to me in this fashion.

And sometimes when I journal, even though I don't consciously gain a new awareness, I just feel better after having had the opportunity to vent.

I now see a direct correlation between how honest I am willing to be in my journal entries and how honest I am willing to be with myself and others in general. I am finding that the more I face the "total" me through my writing—my shadow side as well as my light side—the more I am learning to accept and understand myself and my feelings. It is a process of discovery, of uncovering myself one piece at a time. It is one more step on the road to wholeness.

activity 4

keep a compliment scrapbook

For more than two years I belonged to a group of women that became known as "The Angel Group." Everyone in the group was a seeker. We all wanted to develop our spirituality, and each woman did just that in her own unique way. Some attended organized churches; many didn't. It was a wonderfully supportive group where people could explore their own beliefs as well as share new ideas and attitudes.

One year, for Christmas, we celebrated by filling out "Angel grams" for each other. We completed a slip for each person present, writing down the special qualities we saw in that person. We then exchanged the slips in an atmosphere of camaraderie and love.

About a week after the celebration, I found myself struggling to find a way to recognize my own worth and stop comparing myself with others. Through divine guidance it was suggested to me that I should write down compliments others give me, so that I could reread them and integrate them. It would be a way for me to acknowledge the compliments and learn from them. It was further suggested that I begin by including the Angel grams that I had received. Soon after, I purchased a beautiful scrapbook and began this very enriching experience.

I faithfully followed the guidance I had been given and wrote down the positive things that people said to me. It was a revealing experience. What I learned was that I paid much closer attention to criticism than I did to praise. If someone said something critical about me, I would be able to repeat the statement verbatim a week later. If they complimented me, however, I tended to get embarrassed and afterwards thought, "What was it they said?"

Keeping the scrapbook was a way of reversing those priorities. It required me to focus on my strengths and talents instead of my shortcomings. I had to pay attention to a compliment instead of brushing it off, since I had to write it down when I got home. I began to realize how difficult it was for me to accept praise.

I also began to realize how difficult I had made it for family and friends to compliment me over the years. Because I felt self-conscious about the compliments, I tended to dismiss them and change the subject quickly. It wasn't that I didn't appreciate them; I wanted them desperately. The problem was that I felt unworthy to receive them.

the benefits of keeping a compliment scrapbook

A compliment scrapbook is a wonderful tool for gaining insight into yourself and for understanding how other people see you. I was already pretty well aware of the parts of my personality that my family and friends *didn't* like. (Even though I don't particularly relish hearing these things, I am very grateful for their honesty. I always have a list of things I'm working to improve.)

I didn't, however, have nearly as clear a picture about what people saw as my strengths. After keeping the scrapbook for about a year I started to gain a more accurate idea of what people saw. I started to see patterns in people's comments and found that fascinating. People that didn't even know each other would comment on the same quality. It helped me to be more objective about myself and gain a clearer understanding of myself.

One of the things I most enjoy about my scrapbook is that it enables me to hear people's words when I am comfortable and more receptive. I can savor them in my home office, curled up in my wing-back chair, without the slightest feeling of embarrassment getting in the way. It is easier for me to integrate the words this way.

My compliment scrapbook has also been invaluable to me on more than one occasion when I was going through a particularly trying time and questioning my value to the world. In those "dark nights of the soul" it is incredibly helpful to let the love and nurturing wash over you. Sometimes our loved ones hold the vision of our goodness when we are just not able to see it ourselves.

how to begin

The scrapbook I keep is a standard size—about 13" x 13" with plain white pages. The main criteria in choosing a scrapbook is that it feel pampering to *you*. Choose a quality book that will bring you pleasure when you look at it. Remember that you deserve this!

My book has metal extenders that enable me to purchase additional pages. (I have used many more pages than I ever thought I would.) A scrapbook can contain whatever nourishes your soul. In addition to the compliments, I have included in my scrapbook such things as birthday cards, Mother's Day and Valentine cards, notes from loved ones, newspaper clippings, and a treasured letter of recommendation from a former employer.

In deciding whether or not to include an item, the criteria I use is honesty. I only keep that which I feel truly came from a person's heart. If I think something is the least bit insincere, I leave it out. After all, my goal is to gain a better understanding of myself. I want to do this as accurately as possible.

I write down compliments that people give me as soon as possible to remember their words accurately. If I can't add it to the scrapbook that day, I write the information on a sheet of scrap paper, date the piece of paper, perhaps write a sentence or two of background information regarding the occasion, and then store it in a drawer with the scrapbook.

When I have a day where I feel like I want to pamper myself, I pull the book out and go to work updating it.

There is neither a right way nor a wrong way to keep a compliment scrapbook—only your own unique, wonderful way. It is a personal reflection of its owner and will therefore be unlike any other. It is a celebration of yourself.

After keeping a scrapbook for several years now, I realize that my compliment scrapbook is one of the very best gifts I have ever given myself. It is a source of much pleasure and insight (and at times great comfort).

Keeping up the scrapbook has become second nature to me and is a very enjoyable process. It is making it easier for me to hear loving words and integrate them. I am deeply grateful to Spirit for suggesting that I do this. I have been deeply rewarded for time spent on this endeavor.

activity 5

learn to nurture yourself

One of the biggest differences in my life in the past 20 years is the way I view myself and, because of that, the way I *treat* myself. When I look back at how I treated myself 20 years ago, I now see how very critical I was.

As I have grown in my spiritual awareness, I have begun to realize that not only do we deserve to respect ourselves, but that it is a necessity that we do so. We really *are* supposed to "Love our neighbors as *ourselves.*" We are supposed to love *both* of us.

I am gaining an increased awareness of our connectedness to others and the fact that as we treat others, so will we treat ourselves. As we treat ourselves, so will we treat others. If we are harsh and critical with ourselves, that cannot help but show up in our treatment of others.

developing a new attitude

Treating myself with love and respect has required a significant attitude shift for me. I needed to release the false belief I held about self-nurturing being a form of selfishness and, therefore, sinful.

In the past, I may have appeared to others as though I was treating myself kindly, but the truth is that I wasn't. I didn't listen to myself. I didn't honor my feelings. I didn't enforce healthy boundaries. I chose to persistently make other people's opinions of me more important than my opinion of myself. I constantly nagged myself and told myself that I wasn't as good as other people. It was a recipe for frustration and emotional turmoil.

Gradually, as I began to understand that I *did* have value in the Universe, I started to change my perceptions. I started to seek out people and ideas that would encourage my blossoming sense of self.

One of the best things I did for myself was to ask for a copy of Sarah Ban Breathnach's *Simple Abundance—A Daybook of Comfort and Joy* one Christmas. I found it to be an amazing collection of insights on learning to love and honor yourself.

Ban Breathnach's book includes a short section for each day of the year. I made a commitment to myself to take a few minutes each day to read and think about the material. It turned out to be an incredibly loving thing to do for myself. It slowly and subtly helped me to change the way I saw my place and myself in the world. It was a very meaningful and healing step for me.

stopping the negative self-talk

I have found that one of the most insidious ways in which I have been unloving to myself is in my self-talk. Without realizing it, I had used critical, self-deprecating language toward myself for my entire life. The first step toward changing this long-established pattern came when I chose to become *aware*; to really listen to how I spoke to myself.

I observed that when I made a mistake, I would make fun of myself by saying, "Duh!" I became aware of how incredibly critical that was. Each time I said it, I reinforced in myself the idea that it wasn't permissible to make mistakes — that if I made one I was stupid. I have decided that is most definitely *not* the message I want to give myself, so I now try to avoid saying "duh." If I say it out of habit without thinking, I just try to lovingly remind myself that making mistakes is human and that's the way we learn.

The skill of positive self-talk is one that I am learning slowly and gradually. I have found that it is a habit we can best learn by being unfailingly patient with ourselves. After all, chances are we have lived our entire lives being critical of ourselves. The process requires awareness and effort but the rewards are well worth it!

treating ourselves as we would a friend

It amazes me sometimes just how harsh we can be with ourselves— how unkind in so many little ways. When faced with a situation where I am inclined to judge myself negatively, it helps me a great deal if I can gain a different perspective. The technique I frequently use is viewing the situation as though it involves someone other than myself.

I find I oftentimes have a double standard. If I find myself being judgmental because I have taken time from my schedule to nurture myself, I will think "Would I be that critical of a friend if they did the same thing?" Invariably I will realize that I would view it differently. I know my friends to be intelligent, productive women and know that the time off was helping them recharge their physical, mental, or emotional batteries. When I look at the situation through objective eyes, it often looks very different.

taking time for ourselves each day

Sometimes we can feel so disconnected from ourselves that we don't even know how to get in touch with what we want and who we really are. One of the best ways to rediscover ourselves is to have time dedicated to that pursuit each day.

In this busy world of ours, I realize that finding time for ourselves each day can be a challenge. When we get to the point where we start to recognize that *we* are one of our priorities, it gets a bit easier. When we also remember that our soul development is the reason why we are here to begin with, it gets easier still.

There is no prescribed amount of time you should set aside for your personal time each day. It is dependent upon your particular schedule and commitments. I would recommend a minimum of 15 minutes daily, however.

It is important that it be your time—no phone, no interruptions. A friend of mine who has a 2-year-old daughter gets up before the rest of the family so she can have time to herself. Another friend, the mother of seven, found that her family would honor her privacy when she was in the bathtub, so that is where she meditates. I tend to be a real night owl so I often read and journal late in the evening. It doesn't matter what time of day you choose, as long as you *do* choose to find the time for yourself on a consistent basis.

The very act of deciding *how* to spend your solitary moments is a wonderful step toward getting to know the real you and your own unique preferences. Here are some suggestions just in case you are having concerns about getting started:

- Take a bubble bath
- Go for a walk
- Write in your journal
- Work on your compliment scrapbook
- Read a book
- Just sit and let your mind wander
- Spend time gardening
- Listen to soothing music
- Meditate

The objective of this personal time is to have a few quiet moments to reconnect with yourself. If you are uncomfortable with the process initially, don't be concerned. The more you honor yourself by taking this time, the more comfortable you will become with it. As you learn to temporarily turn away from the world and turn toward your inner self, you will come to value this process. And before you know it, you will begin to deeply treasure these precious moments with your very best friend—you.

activity 6

develop an attitude of gratitude

Several years ago, when I was the director of a volunteer center, I invited Lisa, a director from another state, to visit. I also asked her if she would like to spend the night in our home.

When Lisa and I were saying good night for the evening, she suddenly said to me, "Do you know what a gratitude journal is? I have kept one for the past year and it has changed my life." She went on to say that she viewed her life differently now—looking for the good in it. "I write down five things every evening. During the day I look for things that I can add to the list that night."

I was so moved by Lisa's sincerity that I decided I would likewise try it. For Christmas that year I requested a copy of Sarah Ban Breathnach's companion journal *The Simple Abundance Journal of Gratitude*. Lisa was right. Keeping the gratitude journal did change my life.

I believe the value of a gratitude journal lies in opening a person up to a different perspective. It changes your focus. It is so easy to look for the negative in life—the problems, the things that aren't going right, the apparent lack. A gratitude journal enables you to see that you are, in fact, richly blessed. I found Ban Breathnach's journal to be a perfect way to get started with this process because it discussed the value of being grateful and gave many examples.

Any type of journal could be used for a gratitude journal. The second year I kept one, I wanted more space so I could write about my blessings in greater detail. I chose a hardbound sketchbook at an artist's supply store. It had blank pages and lots of room—exactly what I wanted. If money is tight, you could staple sheets of paper together and make your own book. The book itself is irrelevant; the importance of it lies in the process.

I have found, just like Lisa said, that keeping the gratitude journal has changed my focus. I am much more grateful for my life and the people who share it. It has also been a wonderful way of teaching me to stay in the present moment. When I am totally in the present moment (not thinking about the past or the future), I am most able to appreciate the experience.

Recently, for example, I took a 90-year-old relative shopping for a poinsettia plant. In the past, my mind would have probably been focused elsewhere—perhaps thinking about the remaining errands we wanted to accomplish. This time, instead, as we walked along the rows of the greenhouse, I was aware of this being an incredibly delightful experience. Here I was, listening to Christmas music as I walked with this woman I dearly love, in the midst of literally thousands of beautiful flowers. I was fully in the moment, and it offered me a gift of deep pleasure. It is this deeper awareness of the beauty of everyday moments that a gratitude journal has brought me.

Lisa wrote to me, after she got home, thanking me for the professional help that I had given her. I have since come to realize that she gave me a much greater gift than I gave her. I may have offered her suggestions that would help at this particular job; she offered me a suggestion that has subtly altered my life.

activity 7

create a support system

Relatives, friends, and acquaintances play many different roles in our lives ranging from casual to emotionally intimate. I view each of us as standing in the middle of a garden which has many tiers. The outermost tier consists of people we interact with in a casual manner—the checkout clerk at a large store, the repair person we talk to once a year. As we proceed inward on the tiers of our garden, the relationships become more meaningful. The area closest to us—our innermost tier—encompasses those with whom we can truly be ourselves. With them we are free to express our deepest thoughts, feelings, and dreams.

The people that are in my inner garden are the family members and friends with whom I feel safest. I feel comfortable expressing to them my thoughts and beliefs because, even if they don't agree with me, I know they will respond with respect. They provide a safe place for me to explore my issues. They love me enough to be patient with my process of growth.

I am deeply grateful for these people in my life, especially since I haven't always had relationships that were emotionally intimate. For many years I was so afraid that people would reject me if they knew the *real* me that I refrained from letting people into the inner tier of my garden. I kept them at a safe distance.

developing emotional intimacy

As I look back over my adult life, I recognize people and experiences that have helped teach me about emotional intimacy. Of particular assistance to me were friends who shared my desire for emotional and spiritual growth. Together we consciously worked on establishing an environment of acceptance with each other.

I began to understand that it was just as challenging for others to openly and honestly reveal themselves to me as it was for me to disclose myself to them. I saw them engaging in the same dance as me…revealing a bit of themselves and then stepping back to observe the other person's reaction. Bit by bit, we did less "stepping back." Gradually we learned to trust each other and began sharing the deeper, more hidden, layers of ourselves.

These relationships had a profound effect upon my life. Each time I was able to open myself a little more, delve a little deeper, and be increasingly honest about who I am, I released one more secret, one more piece of shame. Each time I told a confidante who I *really* was— instead of who I thought they wanted to see—and the response I received was acceptance, I took a step toward wholeness.

I think that close, supportive relationships can have tremendous healing benefits. They remind us that we are not alone in this experience of being human; that we are all more similar than not; and that we are loveable despite our sometimes hurtful actions.

Relationships also offer us experiences in which we can develop our own ability to love more deeply. As others share with us the areas of their lives they struggle with, we are given opportunities to choose compassion and understanding instead of judgment. It is a win/win situation. The more we view others as worthy of love, the more we are able to extend that same gentleness to ourselves.

choosing our friends consciously

Not long ago I entered into a thought-provoking discussion on friendship. A woman I had recently met asked me what I look for in friends. In order to answer her more completely, I took time that evening to journal on the subject. I came up with the following list:

1. They are honest, compassionate, trustworthy people who live their lives in constructive ways.
2. They are independent. I am not responsible for their growth, nor are they responsible for mine.
3. They work at developing emotionally intimate relationships.
4. They are open-minded to new ideas and concepts.
5. They have a desire to continually grow and they encourage my growth.
6. They have an empowered (not victim) attitude. They lovingly point out to me when I slip back into the role of victim.
7. They approach life with a sense of humor.
8. They have a quality/qualities that I so admire that I want to be around them in hopes that I can develop more of that trait in myself.

I have found that as I evolve on a personal level, my ideas about friendship have undergone changes as well. I am developing a clearer picture of what a healthy relationship looks like. Sometimes this has necessitated my making changes within existing relationships.

In the past, for instance, I have had more than one friendship in which I found myself in the role of nurturer on a constant basis. The other person looked to me for their well-being. If I wasn't available for them, I felt guilty. I felt responsible for these women and found the relationships to be emotionally draining.

Eventually I began to realize that, in fact, I wasn't being a good friend to them. I *hadn't* been doing these women a favor. Instead, I was encouraging their dependency, teaching them to rely on me. I was sharing in the misperception that they were victims and needed someone to save them. Without even realizing it, I was supporting their belief about their own lack of power.

I now view friendships differently. I have found the best relationships to be those that are based upon equality—where each person takes responsibility for their own growth and own life. I have come to understand that being supportive and nurturing in a relationship is not the same thing as being responsible for someone else's well-being.

My friend Cindy has a theory about friendship being like a savings account. Sometimes you make deposits. Sometimes you make withdrawals. Ideally, it balances out in the long run. I think there is a great deal of wisdom in that.

developing a support system

I would encourage you, on your spiritual journey, to seek out fellow travelers—people who share a commitment to personal growth. These relationships hold the potential for great healing for both of you. It has been my experience that my friends are often mirrors for me. Time and time again I have worked to help a friend become clear on an issue only to realize afterwards that there was great value in the conversation for me as well.

If you decide that you would like to bring more supportive relationships into your life, begin by asking Spirit to guide you to people who would assist in your growth as you assist in theirs. Ask that these relationships be for the highest good of all.

You may be surprised. You may have relationships right now that have the potential to be deeper and more rewarding. Or you may be led to search out people/groups that share your desire to consciously evolve.

I have found personal growth and metaphysical classes to be a helpful source for meeting like-minded people. Area bookstores sometimes contain information regarding classes offered in a community. The employees there may be able to recommend magazines, newspapers, or organizations that will be of interest to you. As you begin to network, have faith; Spirit will work with you to bring you who and what you need.

activity 8

invite guidance through automatic writing

I was initially exposed to automatic writing many years ago when I heard others talk about the process and its potential for spiritual guidance. In 1990, at the retreat I have attended for a number of years, I participated in a weeklong class on "listening to inner guidance." The instructor, B.J. King, explained the process of automatic writing and the benefits of receiving this direct communication from Spirit.

Automatic writing entails quieting ourselves and creating a peaceful, receptive frame of mind. We enter into the process with the intention of *listening*—to God, our Higher Self, and other helpful spiritual beings.

The purpose of automatic writing is to establish a direct channel of communication with Spirit. This process helps us learn how to be more aware of inner guidance and begin trusting it. (It also helps eliminate the error that is possible when information comes through a third party.) In automatic writing, we have the opportunity to not only receive guidance, but to actually *feel* the unconditional love that Spirit has for us.

automatic writing compared to journaling

The process of automatic writing is very different from that of journaling. In journaling, *we* are the creator of what is written. Often, it gushes out and is cathartic. The intention is to express ourselves—to release feelings and thoughts by writing them down. In automatic writing, we are not the creator; we are the receiver. The information does not originate with us. We are in the role of a secretary objectively writing down the words of another.

Journaling is done in the first person: "I feel the need to explore what is troubling me today." Automatic writing is done in the second person. Instead of being the speaker, we are the one being spoken to: "You are our beloved. It is a pleasure to work with you." The messages do not come *from* us; they are flowing *through* us.

understanding the process

To begin the process of automatic writing, you quiet yourself, place yourself in a meditative state, and ask Spirit for guidance. You can ask a question if you like, or you can ask for whatever general guidance would be for your highest good. You then write down whatever comes to you. The information comes *through* you but not *from* you.

I suspect that each person's experience with automatic writing would be unique to them. I am open to whatever guidance will be for my highest good at that particular time and have been given messages from the angelic realm and my guides. Oftentimes I feel the loving presence of my mother and brother, Norm. The energy—the essence—of each being is different so I am able to tell them apart. I do not choose who comes to me; they come of their own accord when they wish to tell me something.

The subject matter of messages I receive varies with the day and the spiritual energy that is communicating with me. The common thread that runs through all the messages I have received, however, is Spirit's great love for mankind. Their guidance is never harsh or critical. It is always given in a reassuring, loving, supportive manner.

how I go about it

I approach my automatic writing with an intention to **listen**—to be receptive to the guidance of Spirit. I have found that this necessitates my being open; suspending judgment while I do the writing; and putting down my defenses and my walls. In short, it necessitates *trusting*.

When I sit down to write, I make sure that I am in a place where I will not be disturbed. If noise is a problem, I use a set of earplugs. I turn off the ringer to the telephone and light a candle.

Before I begin the process, I take time to ask God to allow only spiritual communication from high-level, evolved spiritual beings— communication that would be for my highest good. I then become very relaxed so that my mind can quiet itself. To do this, I use a cassette tape from B.J. King that aids in the process of preparing myself. The tape helps me relax and get into a receptive mindset, but a tape is not vital to this technique—willingness to receive guidance is the only requirement.

During this process I try to keep my mind as free from my own thoughts as possible. I do not physically "hear" words from Spirit. Instead, I experience the process as words coming into my mind; thoughts that did not originate with me. I write them down as quickly as possible without judging them. If I start to question whether I am actually receiving the words or making them up, I remind myself that there is plenty of time to decide that later.

King recommends that a person new to the process write with a pencil due to its being made of an organic material. She has found that it facilitates the process for beginners. Once the flow is intact, a person can easily progress to a computer if desired.

messages I have received

Over the years that I have been doing automatic writing, I have received many messages. Some are several pages long and some are less than a page. (The length depends upon how much time I have that particular day to devote to the process.) I have found Spirit always willing to communicate with me. My challenge has been to become receptive and quiet enough to let their words flow through me.

The following italicized sections are excerpts taken from messages I have received. In some, I have quoted an entire paragraph; from others, only a couple of lines. Most often the guidance I receive addresses specific issues in my own life. Many of the excerpts that I have included here are a bit broader in scope, as I believe that they are applicable to other people as well.

I believe we are *all* deeply and dearly loved by Spirit. I believe we are *all* given unconditional support and guidance if we take the time, and make the effort, to hear it.

In one of my very first messages I received:

*We love you. We are here to help and guide you. We will show you many things. You **are** a child of the universe. Death means nothing. The flow of life goes on and on forever. It is not diminished by death.*

Don't be judgmental of the content of what you are writing. Opening the channels of communication is the important thing. It is a process you will learn and become more and more comfortable with. You have asked to be open to direction and so it is. We are here to help and guide you.

You have many who are watching over you and want to be of assistance to you. Allow them to help. We watch over you and guide you and will continue to do so. We are very pleased that you recognize (value) us and are coming to us. Be open to the process and just allow it. You will be convinced as time goes on. You will know the truth.

A few days later I received:

You are on the right path. You desire spiritual knowledge. It will be shown to you as you progress.

Your mother loves you very much. She is with you often. You are very dear to her. You are doing well and she is very proud of you. You are learning to communicate with her. You are putting away negativity. That is a barrier that prevents communication. You are learning to let the words flow. You will benefit much from this.

Your brother Norm wants you to know that he is also with you and loves you very much. He is pleased with the path you are choosing. He looks forward to communicating with you. He has much to tell you. He wants to assure you of his love.

In the beginning, thoughts of, "Am I just making this all up?" constantly ran through my mind as I did the automatic writing. The most difficult part of the process for me was learning to allow the flow of thoughts through my mind, out my hand, and onto the paper without judging them. I found this to be very challenging. My mind constantly generated questions of doubt. I had a difficult time believing that I was worthy of having Spirit speak to me.

It took a lot of perseverance to continue the writing when my negativity and doubt were so strong. Spirit continually encouraged my efforts and explained to me how the negativity stopped the flow. With their reassurance, I continued the process even though I still questioned my own ability to do this.

Allow the flow. You are doing a good job. We are pleased with your progress and your willingness to be open. Continue the process. It will flow more and more easily as time goes on.

Your life is divinely inspired. You have let us know that you are open to guidance and therefore we are responding. You can trust this guidance. Be at peace. We will show you the way if you stay open to our words. Have faith in us to help you.

And, on another occasion:

You are making progress. Continue to do so and we will continue to show you the path. It is not mysterious. It is developing as you develop. We are here to support these endeavors and shine light upon your path. Believe in your abilities. Low self-esteem will inhibit your being able to reach your potential. Work on loving and accepting yourself as we love and accept you. Continue to study and pray and meditate. The steps (and the course) will be shown you.

*It is **very important** that you turn inward and trust the guidance there instead of looking for it outwardly. That which is outward can supplement, and validate, what you get but the greatest truth lies within you. We are anxious and willing to guide you and this gives us a much clearer form of expression. We are very appreciative of that.*

I received the following on a day when I was struggling with my self-worth in general:

Do know that you are our beloved. You have been very judgmental and harsh with yourself this week so work on releasing that. You are the one judging yourself; not us. We love you and accept you as you are.

Work on releasing the negativity about yourself. It holds you back in many areas and prevents you from full development. I have created you with specific plans in mind. Trust that I am with you and am involved in your life. I will help you to develop. You do not need to do it all yourself. Put your hand in mine. You have but to ask and I help you.

I will show you my plan—do not fear. The most important lesson is to realize that you are important and significant to me and you do have a part to play—a role; a job; in many ways and in many situations. I will be able to work with and through you. Do not let your sense of your unworthiness stop this process. You have much potential. You are my child and I am your parent. You are beautiful in my eyes and the eyes of others. Do you not think that I will help you if you ask?

Do not be concerned that these messages I am giving you are not "profound" in your eyes. They are what you need to hear at the present time. Establishing the link is of the utmost importance at the present. Building up the trust. You are learning the process. Relax and be at peace with the process.

I love you…I love you.

On one occasion I was feeling frustrated with what I observed in the world and felt powerless to do anything about it. When I asked for guidance, I received the following:

*It is best for you not to get overwhelmed. It is in impacting your "corner" of the world, and joining with others doing the same, that change on a mass level is made. What you do **does** matter. It does impact consciousness as a whole. You are impacting negative situations that are/may be present in the world.*

*Do not be overwhelmed. You are not alone; your positive energy is joining with the energy of many others. Together you **will** effect the change you desire. All you are responsible for is your piece of the puzzle. There is divine order in what is going on, whether or not it looks like it on the surface.*

Continue to ask for our help and guidance and trust that it is being given you, for it is. You have a very strong support system in the heavenly realms and we work in conjunction with you in these matters.

You are not being deserted so have no fear of that. We love you more dearly and more completely than words could ever say and we very much care about your well-being. You are not "going the course" unaided or unguided. You are, in fact, watched over every minute of every day with each of your very breaths.

I have received guidance on a variety of different subjects. The following message was in regard to my struggling with my eating habits:

We wish to speak with you about a matter at hand. We know it is of concern to you and we seek to bring you comfort. We are, of course, talking about the issue of your weight. You will not always struggle with this. You have emotions—primarily sadness—to release. Your inner being is agitated and trying to comfort itself in the best (or most familiar) way that it knows how at the present.

When the sadness is released you will feel much less compulsion to eat. Do know that we are with you every step of the way during this process and we definitely see long term success. It is, of course, your choice to make but we know the true dreams of your heart and physical health is one of them. We will make your path easier; make sure you remember to call on us when you need help in this matter.

In response to asking about the well-being of my mother, I received:

> *Your mother has progressed nicely and is working on her own learning. She has progressed much since the incarnation she shared with you. She very much honors the time she had with you and acknowledges the part you played in each other's growth.*
>
> *She continues to love you deeply and assures you that she always will. You chose this lifetime together because of the eternal love you share. It began eons before this lifetime and will continue for eons more into eternity. Have no doubt you will be joined together again and there will be a wondrous reunion.*

Time and time again, Spirit is gentle and loving with me when I most need it:

> *You are in a very fragmented state today. We are glad you have come to us. That is the perfect time to contact us. Do not feel that you have to "have your act together" before you can consult us. It is what we are here for—to give you aid and assistance in times when you are feeling "befuddled."*

looking back at the process

When I first began doing the automatic writing, it took a number of sessions for me to feel familiar with it. It was a very different process than the journaling that I was so accustomed to, where *I* was the author of the words. As I practiced this technique of receiving, however, it became more and more comfortable to me.

Eventually, I found that if I set the written material aside and read it the next day (instead of immediately after writing it), I was more objective about its origin. As time went on, and I had more and more experiences with the writing, I began to realize that I could trust the process—that I was receiving guidance.

When I now reread old entries, I realize even more how very helpful the guidance has been to me. I have been given suggestions in dealing with problems, insights that I may not have otherwise gotten, and constant encouragement. And, as they predicted, the process is helping me learn to trust myself. It is helping me go within for my guidance and use outside help as a supplement and validation.

When I look back on the pages and pages of messages I have received over the last ten years, I am amazed at the incredible love and support Spirit has expressed. Many times it has moved me to tears. It is so incredibly gentle; so incredibly understanding:

> We value you far beyond the way you value yourself because we see you much more accurately than you see yourself. We are always there. And it is our pleasure to do so. It is a labor of love. Take a deep breath, little one, and feel our energy fill your lungs, our love envelop you.

For their guidance and their ever-present compassion, I am deeply grateful.

activity 9

establish a sacred space

I have greatly benefited from the creation of a sacred space in my home. I had wanted a place of my own where I could do spiritual work: a spot where I could read, meditate, write, and study. When we turned a spare bedroom into a home office, using part of the room for my sacred space became a priority to me.

The area I decided upon was not very large, but I made it very efficient. I thought carefully about the items that I wanted to include: a chair that made me feel pampered and cozy; a small chairside table that I could put meaningful items on; a good light for reading; a nearby cassette player so I could listen to relaxing tapes. I also included in this room a bookcase where I could keep many of the books that I so love and that have been of such wonderful assistance to me.

In hindsight, the most important thing I did to prepare my space was to ask for angelic assistance in the creation of it. I asked their guidance each step of the way from choosing the style of the chair to the items that would be placed on the table. The end result is a room that I absolutely love to be in.

creating your own space

There is no prescribed way to create a sacred space. There are many variables. What kind of space is available in your apartment or home? Is it large or small? Will you need to share this space with others? If your living area is small, could you carve out a place in your bedroom or another room where you would be comfortable?

Begin by trying to discover what would most nurture you in your space. Do you want a place to read? to meditate? to write? to listen to music? to pray? to just sit and think? What items would you like to be surrounded with? candles? photographs? crystals? fresh flowers? What colors and textures bring you the most pleasure? I have a cozy throw draped over the back of my chair. It is perfect for those times when I am feeling chilly or just want to be wrapped in something comforting.

The most important aspect of a sacred space is that it honor you. It will be a space where you will do some of the most important work of your life, so let it nurture you. Think about the items that you feel most pamper you and incorporate them into the space. If you were creating a physical space for God in your home, would you not take the time to make it as special as possible? *You* are a part of God and you deserve no less.

the benefits of a sacred space

My sacred space is both practical and nurturing. I am deeply grateful for it. I use it every day. I no longer feel like a nomad wandering around my house looking for a quiet place to read or write.

When I am in my sacred space I am reminded that I am valuable. Making the decision to incorporate this special study/meditating/writing area into our home office was a statement of worthiness about myself. By creating it, I sent myself the message "You *are* important. Your inner work has great value." That is a powerful message that applies to each of us.

activity 10

make peace with your parents *and* yourself

If you still have unresolved issues with your parents (and how common this is!) you are keeping both yourself *and* them in bondage. You have the power within you, if you so choose, to set all of you free. When I first started working on my relationship with my father, I did it as a gift to him. It ended up being a gift to *me*.

I don't know how I would have begun to find peace in my relationship with my father if I had not, at the same time, worked on healing my own inner child issues. I found it to be the foundation for learning how to let my father "off the hook." As I began to realize that I didn't need to be dependent upon him for my sense of emotional well-being, I could begin to see him in a much more objective light. It freed me up, for the first time in my life, to begin truly loving him.

acknowledging what is really going on

To deny the existence of our inner child is to handicap ourselves in understanding the dynamics that play out on a daily basis in our life. The patterns that we established in our childhood are our "default settings": the ways of thinking and acting that are so much a part of us that we revert to them automatically. They remain strong within us as adults unless we consciously set about releasing them.

These patterns will vary a great deal in intensity depending on the particular environment in which we were raised. If we were exposed to a great deal of criticism as children, our inner critical parent will be strong. As we become adults our inner critical parent picks up precisely where our parents, society, and the other adults in our childhood left off. We now harangue our own inner child. We now make ourselves feel defective and unworthy.

Another very important aspect of our internal dialogue is our inner nurturing parent. It is that part of the self that is supportive, loving, and kind. It is the aspect of us that has internalized the loving, positive messages we received as a child. It is the inner nurturing parent that has the power to heal.

Our inner nurturing parent is the one that says, "Wow, I really did a good job!" when we complete something we are proud of. It is the voice that whispers words of encouragement and comfort. For some, the voice is strong. For others, the voice is but a mere whisper, rarely heard. One of the things that I have worked diligently on is strengthening this part of myself.

a meaningful step

One of the things I did while I was working on my inner child issues was to keep a journal dedicated exclusively to the work. It turned out to be very helpful for me. A friend had given me a beautiful journal by Sue Patton Thoele called *The Courage to Be Yourself Journal* and this was what I used, although any journal would work.

I thought this particular journal was very appropriate for the inner child work I was doing because it took exactly that—a great deal of courage—to do the work. It involved many steps and many tearful, emotional entries in which I poured forth the anger, frustration, and pain I felt from my childhood.

My initial goal in keeping this inner child journal was to get in touch with my feelings regarding my relationship with my father. Because I had such a strong pattern of intellectualizing his actions instead of focusing on the emotions they engendered in me, I wrote the following very prominently on the inside cover of my journal:

Every time I come into this space, I will abide by one guideline: not only is it not desirable to explain away my father's actions, it is actually not permitted. If I start to do so, I will be missing the goal of this experience…to listen fully to my child within.

The journal gave me a space to explore the particular dynamics that had influenced my childhood. I gained much-needed objectivity through the process of writing these dynamics down. The journal was also a wonderful place for me to record my victories—times when I *did* listen to my inner child and took one more step toward making peace with her.

developing our inner nurturing parent

During my process of inner child work, I found it a necessity to strengthen my internal nurturing parent. Sometimes I needed to envision this parent as being masculine; at other times feminine.

When I was working through addressing long-held emotions regarding my father, I found it extremely beneficial to work with this masculine inner parent. At times, in addition to my journaling, I had a great need to "talk" to this nurturing father within. I did so by creating a safe space for myself.

I envisioned, in my mind, a room where I could go and speak with a gentle, kindly man with whom I felt very safe. I felt much loved by him. This nurturing father gave me permission to express the feelings that I experienced so much guilt over. The process was extremely nurturing and healing for me. He was the sensitive, gentle father that I had always longed for.

At other times I felt the need to be in the presence of my feminine inner parent. I welcomed her softness, her understanding, her wisdom. I saw her as being both empowered and compassionate and I appreciated her unconditional love.

learning to listen

Working with our inner child is an ongoing process. The more I work with these inner aspects of myself (the inner child, the critical parent, the nurturing parent/s), the easier it is becoming for me to recognize the roles each of them play. When I am upset about an issue or a situation, I am learning to momentarily turn my attention away from the outer world and quietly focus on the drama that is going on within me.

Frequently, I become aware of the inner critical parent voicing harsh judgments about me. At other times, my inner child is agitated about a perceived problem and wants to be heard. I try to envision my inner nurturing mother setting the child on her lap, looking into her eyes, and saying, "What do you want to tell me?"

I am surprised at how difficult this process is at times. It amazes me how threatening it can feel to really listen to the child. At those times I remind myself that I do not have to act upon the child's desires; I only have to listen to her.

Sometimes my inner child will need to express herself by writing down her feelings. At other times, she needs an extended period of being "held" and comforted and gently spoken to. Occasionally, the lone act of listening is enough to soothe her. Once she knows that she is being heard—really being listened to—her agitation often starts to subside.

responding to the child within

I have come to realize that how I relate to the different aspects of myself depends upon the particular situation. Sometimes, when my inner child is upset, I am able to see myself as the inner nurturing parent and visualize comforting the child. Other times, when I am more deeply upset, I identify more closely with the child. I *am* the child and the one in need of soothing.

During those instances when I feel I *am* the child, I find it helpful to make myself physically comfortable (e.g. snuggled in bed or in a cozy chair). I then find it calming to play music that "speaks" to me. My favorite cassette tape at times like these is *Songs for the Inner Child* by Shaina Noll. It is a wonderful collection of songs that soothe and nourish.

As I listen to Shaina's songs, I envision myself as a young child being sung to by her parents. I particularly appreciate the fact that in one of the songs Shaina's husband, Richard, sings. It is especially meaningful to me to have a "daddy" sing these soft words of love.

Once I realized how much I could be comforted by music, I started to look for other songs that would also be beneficial. As I listened to my inner child I started becoming aware of popular songs that she responded to. I decided to make a tape of several songs as they played on the radio.

Some of the songs I find most nurturing are Garth Brooks' "To Make You Feel My Love," Michael Bolton's "In the Arms of Love," and Phil Collin's "True Colors." If you choose to create a personal tape for your own inner child, you could ask her to help you in choosing the music. She will let you know what she finds helpful.

choosing differently

Learning to be sensitive to my inner child has made a huge difference in my life. We are not powerless. We are not sentenced to a life of viewing ourselves the way our parents viewed us. We don't have to perpetuate the patterns that were established when we were children.

The first step is to educate ourselves. I again mention the books *Your Inner Child of the Past* by W. Hugh Missildine, M.D., and *Making Peace With Your Parents* by Harold H. Bloomfield, M.D., because these books were so very helpful for me. I needed to gain an understanding of the dynamics at play in my life and these books greatly contributed to my doing so.

You may also wish to acquire a copy of John Bradshaw's book, *Homecoming.* I found this book very helpful. One of the things I appreciated about this particular book was that it helped me develop a strong sense of my inner nurturing parent(s). This was extremely useful as I set about the process of healing my inner child.

changing our internal climate

We each have an internal emotional climate. Much like the weather outdoors, it can be either stormy or calm. The interaction of these three aspects of ourselves—the inner child, the inner critical parent, and the inner nurturing parent—helps determine what our internal emotional climate will be.

I now realize that I can choose to have my inner nurturing parent take a much more active role in my internalized dialogues. As I do this, the inner critical parent that used to dominate most of my thoughts is weakening. I am choosing to empower one parent over the other. I am finding that as I bring more of this loving, nurturing presence into my life, my emotional climate is changing. I now have many more bright, sunny days.

activity 11

open your mind to working with angels and other spirit beings

I consider it a great gift and honor to work with the angels. It brings me guidance, assistance, and a wonderful feeling of connection with spirit beings. I also know that my being able to work with them is not based upon my being special; it is based upon my being willing. That is the only requirement. It truly is as simple as that.

The hurdle to overcome (if we have one) lies not in their being unavailable. The hurdle usually lies in our unwillingness to be able to accept anything that our five senses cannot validate for us. Angels *do* exist. We reach out to them when we open our minds to the possibility that maybe they *are*, in fact, real. We reach out to them when we consider the possibility that perhaps *we are worthy of their help.*

It is my understanding that angels have specific skills just as we humans do, so I often request the assistance of particular angels. If I am entering onto a busy highway, for instance, and concerned about merging into rush-hour traffic, I ask the driving angels to help me. If I am involved with a redecorating project I request angels of creativity and beauty. When I pray for my children I call upon the assistance of protective angels.

It has been my experience that angels are more than willing to work with us. When I first started experimenting with working with these light beings I was embarrassed to call upon them for mundane matters. I have found through experience, however, that they are more than happy to help in any circumstance.

My sister Shirley, for instance, calls upon a "parking angel." Time and time again my nieces and I have been in the car with her when an angelic helper will lead her to a convenient, empty parking space in what looked to be a completely filled lot. All we have to do is trust and remember to ask for their assistance.

help with communication

Angels are not our only source of spiritual help. Some people are more comfortable calling upon God; some call upon their own Higher Self, guides, or their Guardian Angel.

As we follow our own unique path we open ourselves, if we so desire, to relationships with many beings of light. I suspect the important thing is that we learn to do the calling and develop the open-mindedness that it takes to recognize Spirit's presence.

One of the most powerful areas of help to me personally has been in the area of communication. I have come to depend deeply on Spirit's willingness to aid my communication with others. Time and time again I have been assisted in meetings and difficult conversations by taking the time to pray and prepare the room in advance.

I do this by asking for guidance, then imagining a thick band of white light around the entire room. (This enhances truthful communication.) I ask that the room be filled with the white light of Christ (God energy). I also ask that the conversation that takes place be for the highest good of everyone involved. I affirm my intention to be a channel of light, love, healing, empowerment, and peace. If I have a particular concern, I will ask for guidance regarding that also.

I have been amazed, time and again, at the difference it makes when I ask for spiritual guidance in communication. I have had this experience of divine help so many times now that I have come to deeply trust it.

give the process time

I find that it becomes easier for me to work with Spirit as time goes on. I suspect that is because I am learning to trust the process. As I have more and more experiences of divine help, it has become much easier to trust that I will receive it.

I would recommend to someone who is just beginning this process to have patience. When I first began experimenting on working with the angels I didn't *always* see an answer to a request I had made. I still don't see an obvious answer every single time. In some situations, it will only be after a period of time has passed that I can recognize their assistance.

It would have been easy initially to become negative and stop trying to develop a relationship with the angels. (Thank heavens, I didn't.) I don't know why my requests didn't always come to pass. In hindsight I wonder if the angels may have tried to nudge me in the right direction and I wasn't sensitive enough yet to feel their guidance. Or maybe they knew my request wasn't in my best interest, even if *I* thought it was.

As I have worked with spiritual beings over the years, though, I have had so many experiences of their guidance and help that I have become a believer. We just have to remember to ask. Working with them has been very rewarding and I am deeply grateful for their presence in my life.

activity 12

give *yourself* the gift
of forgiveness

Some time ago I received the following email from a friend. The author
was unknown.

The Weight of Resentments

A teacher once told each of her students to bring a clear plastic bag and
a sack of potatoes to school. For every person they refused to forgive in their
life's experience, they chose a potato, wrote on it the person's name and the
date, and put it in the plastic bag. Some of their bags were quite heavy.

They were then told to carry this bag with them everywhere for one week,
putting it beside their bed at night, on the car seat when driving, next to their
desk at work.

The hassle of lugging this around with them made it clear what a weight
they were carrying spiritually. This was a great metaphor for the price we pay
for holding onto our pain and heavy negativity. Too often we think of
forgiveness as a gift to the other person, while it is clearly for ourselves!

When I read this story I was impressed with the wonderful way the
teacher had demonstrated to her students the need for forgiveness. Too
often we are under the impression that our holding on to a grudge hurts

the *other* person. In truth, *we* are the ones that are hurt; *we* are the ones that carry it around.

When we have a grievance against someone, we give up power in our lives; power to control the kind of day we are going to have and the mood we are going to be in. When we consciously hold on to a grievance against another person, we shut down a part of our heart. That act has an effect on all of our relationships.

the process of forgiving

In the last few years, I have learned a great deal about the need for forgiveness…for both others and myself. As I consciously work on the issue of forgiveness, I am learning more about it. I share the following insights with you in hopes that they might assist you as well:

1. ***We can't heal grievances we don't acknowledge.*** Grievances come in all sizes—large and small—but each of them takes away from our peace of mind. When I first read the story about the teacher asking her students to consider how many potatoes (grievances) they were carrying around, I remember asking myself the same question. It seemed to me, at the time, that my load was limited to one or two big potatoes. Upon closer examination (and perhaps a deeper level of truth with myself), I realize now that I have carried around a great number of potatoes in my lifetime.

2. ***Forgiveness is not a feeling—forgiveness is a choice.*** Sometimes it is easy to forgive. (A friend or relative, for instance, says something to me and my feelings get hurt. I address it with them and realize that I was misinterpreting what they were saying. Afterwards I am easily able to release the situation.)

   Sometimes, it is difficult to forgive. I have come to understand that forgiveness is not a feeling—forgiveness is a choice. It is a decision we make because we want to set ourselves free. It is a "fork in the road" whereby we choose the quality of life we will live. With a deeply painful issue, this may be a choice that we make numerous times. Each time a different aspect of the situation comes up, we again make the conscious decision, "I choose to forgive you, (name)."

3. **We don't have to do this alone.** When I am feeling "wronged against" (as my children used to say when they were young), the most beneficial step I can take is to ask the assistance of Spirit. I ask that I be able to perceive the person or situation as Spirit does. I ask to be given a *willingness* to forgive. The *desire to be willing* is all Spirit needs to be able to work with us.

4. **We have to feel our pain before we can heal it.** In order to forgive, I must first experience the emotion I have about a situation…the anger, the frustration, the hurt. I need to know that I am being heard. Sometimes I need to do this with the other person involved; sometimes by myself. If I try to skip this process, the emotional pain remains stored within me and the grievance resurfaces in my mind time and time again.

5. **Understanding another's actions can be incredibly beneficial.** *A Course In Miracles* states that people's actions are either an expression of love or an expression of fear. I believe that. After releasing the emotion I feel about a troubling experience, I make a conscious effort to stand back and view the situation from a different perspective…through the eyes of the other person. I have learned that taking time to understand the fears that prompted the other person's actions can make a huge difference in my willingness to forgive.

6. **Remembering the big picture empowers us.** I have found that one of the most beneficial steps I can take in healing a strained relationship is to remember that I am not a victim—that on a soul level I chose this situation because it offers me an opportunity for growth. In any experience, the most important question I can ask myself is, "What is my soul trying to teach me through this encounter?" The more

consciously I can understand the lesson I learned from a painful experience, the more easily I can forgive and release it.

7. **Forgiving *does not mean having unhealthy boundaries*.** Forgiving does not diminish the importance of having healthy boundaries in our lives. Sometimes, after forgiving someone, we come to the conclusion that it is not healthy for us mentally, physically, or emotionally to continue a close relationship with that person. If so, it is important for us to honor that insight. Oftentimes the lesson our soul is trying to teach us is one of self-love. If that necessitates keeping a safe distance from someone, then that is what we must do.

an on-going process

In the last few years, I have made a concerted effort at working on forgiving people in my life. The process is certainly not finished. Rather, I have found that forgiveness is an ongoing course of action and that it requires constant vigilance on my part.

Sometimes my grievances catch me by surprise. I might be talking to someone, for instance, and find myself complaining about someone else. More than once I have thought, "Wow, I had no idea I was harboring that resentment. I really need to work on that."

We don't ever get over the need to work on forgiving. It is a life-long process. Opportunities for grievances pop up on a daily basis in our lives. The challenge is to recognize them and to ask Spirit for the willingness to forgive—and release—them.

learning to forgive ourselves

One of the surprising things I learned, as I started making a very conscious effort to release grievances, is that one of the people I most need to forgive is myself. Oftentimes, as I go through my steps toward forgiving someone else, I will find that I contributed to the situation just as much as they did. As I look at the experience through their eyes, I realize that my actions were equally as hurtful to them as theirs were to me.

I am learning to say, "I'm sorry." I am learning to take more responsibility in the role I play in **their** feeling hurt. I'm also learning to forgive myself for staying in relationships that weren't always emotionally healthy for me. I did the best I knew how at the time. It's important now to forgive myself and let the past go.

What I am observing is that, as I work on forgiving myself, it is becoming easier to forgive others. Conversely, as I work on forgiving others, it is becoming easier for me to forgive myself. What a wonderful benefit!

the key to happiness

Forgiveness is a choice. It is a decision. It is a path that many choose not to take. Oftentimes it is easy to recognize these dear souls as they continue to be miserable about experiences that may have occurred years before. Their minds and their spirits are burdened by the emotional weight of the potatoes they carry.

As I walk down the path of forgiveness, I am experiencing deep changes within myself. I *feel* different. I am more easy-going, more playful, less burdened. As I work on releasing grievances from the past, I find I am more able to live in the present. I have received remarkable healing benefits from the process of forgiveness.

I think back now to the conversation I had many years ago with a relative, in which I said, "You don't understand. I just want to feel better." Little did I know at that time that the answer to feeling better didn't lie outside of myself. Little did I know that *I* held the key to the emotional freedom I so desperately desired.

epilogue

The man who removes a mountain begins by carrying away small stones.

Chinese proverb

Before I began my journey of healing I used to look at myself and think, "I'm really a mess!" I believed that I was the only one who felt that way. I constantly compared myself to others and thought that I wasn't as good. The more I thought I was defective, the more I isolated myself and covered up my true feelings because of shame and embarrassment.

Now, all these years later, I realize that I am not defective; what I am is a soul who has very bravely decided to experience being human. I have come to realize that I am no different than other people—that we all, to a greater or lesser degree, face issues of self-worth. I now know that we *all* struggle at times with the lessons we have come to learn.

Occasionally I will hear someone explain their actions by saying, "You know, you can't teach an old dog new tricks." I couldn't disagree more. We are all capable of change—regardless of our age. The issue isn't whether or not we are *capable* of change; the issue is whether or not we are *willing* to change.

As we progress through this experience of life we have a most important decision to make. We must choose between seeing ourselves as helpless victims of fate, or the empowered co-creators that we really are. If we choose the latter, we give ourselves a great gift. We embark upon a journey of discovering our true identities and our true potential. We embark upon a journey of healing.

I have developed a deep respect for this experience that we are all going through. The very fact that we are even here signifies the incredible courage of our soul—the nobility, the beauty. I am convinced that one of the most important things we can do to assist ourselves in this process is to be gentle with ourselves. We are, after all, children learning to walk.

It is my sincere hope that this book will help you to remember that you are not on this journey alone. I—and countless others—are walking right beside you, each trying our best to learn our soul's lessons. It is encouraging and comforting to know that Spirit also walks with us.

It has been an honor for me to be able to share this book with you. I enclose, within its covers, my deepest love and best wishes for you as you bravely make the changes you desire. And in those dark nights of the soul, when you ask yourself, "What good am I without my cheesecake recipe?" I hope you will find your answers.

Love and Light,
Virginia Sobel

suggested books, tapes and CDs

angelic guidance

Hubbs, Juliet Jaffray and Monaco, Nora. *Universal Cards*, An AngelStar Production, 1994 (book/card set)

Mark, Barbara and Griswold, Trudy. *Angelspeake*, Simon & Schuster, 1995

Sharp, Sally. *100 Ways to Attract Angels*, Trust Publishing, 1994

Young-Sowers, Meredith L. *Angelic Messenger Cards*, Stillpoint, 1993 (book/card set)

automatic writing

Cassette tape to facilitate automatic writing can be ordered from: Namaste Inc., P.O. Box 22174, Oklahoma City, OK, 73123 Phone: 405-773-5210

boundary issues

Katherine, Anne. *Boundaries: Where You End and I Begin*, Fireside/Parkside, 1991

Katherine, Anne. *Where to Draw the Line: How to Set Healthy Boundaries Every Day*, Simon and Schuster, 2000

fear issues

Jeffers, Susan. *Feel The Fear And Do It Anyway*, Fawcett Columbine Book, 1987

inner child work

Bradshaw, John. *Homecoming: Reclaiming and Championing Your Inner Child*, Bantam, 1990

Missildine, M.D., W. Hugh. *Your Inner Child of the Past*, Pocket Books, 1963

Noll, Shaina. *Songs for the Inner Child*, Singing Heart Productions, 1992 (cassette/CD)

journaling

Ban Breathnach, Sarah. *The Simple Abundance Journal of Gratitude*, Warner Books, 1996 (journal)

Forrest, Jan. *Coming Home to Ourselves*, Heart to Heart Press, 1999

Thoele, Sue Patton. *The Courage to Be Yourself Journal*, Conari Press, 1996

parenting issues

Bloomfield, M.D., Harold H. and Felder, Ph.D., Leonard. *Making Peace With Your Parents*, Ballantine Books, 1983

personal growth

Ban Breathnach, Sarah. *Simple Abundance: A Daybook of Comfort and Joy*, Warner Books, 1995

Edelman, Hope. *Motherless Daughters*, Delta, 1994

Hyde, Laura V. *Gifts of the Soul*, Sustainable Solutions Press, 1997

Hyde, Laura V. *The Intimate Soul*, Sustainable Solutions Press, 2001

Forrest, Jan. *Awakening the Spirit Within*, Heart to Heart Press, 2000

Hay, Louise. *You Can Heal Your Life*, Hay House, 1984

Jampolsky, M.D., Gerald G. *Love Is Letting Go Of Fear*, Celestial Arts, 1979

Lara, Adair. *Slowing Down in a Speeded Up World*, Conari Press, 1994

Nuyens, Kay. *Invitation to Greatness*, Changing Focus Press 2002

Peck, M.D., M. Scott. *The Road Less Traveled*, Touchstone, 1978

Stanfield, Jana. *Brave Faith*, Jana StanTunes Music, 1999 (2 CD set)

Zukav, Gary. *The Seat of the Soul*, Simon and Schuster, 1989

Zukav, Gary. *Soul Stories*, Simon and Schuster, 2000

self talk
Helmstetter, Shad. *What To Say When You Talk to Your Self*, Grindle Press, 1986

Virginia Sobel received a B.A. in Education from Michigan State University and has been teaching in a variety of capacities ever since. In addition to her work as an author, Sobel designs and conducts personal growth workshops. Her Self-Esteem Workshop is a powerful six-session course that helps participants develop genuine self-love. Her insights and deep empathy make her a natural-born teacher.

Through her writing and teaching, Sobel reaches out to all who are challenged by painful life experiences, and compassionately shares the lessons, techniques, and activities she has found invaluable in her own healing process. Her experience with suicide, loss, and an emotionally distant father—in concert with the extensive healing work she has undertaken—make her uniquely qualified to assist others in transforming their lives.

Virginia Sobel is the founder of Spirit Whispers, an organization dedicated to personal healing. She is also a Reiki Master, using the Japanese energy-balancing technique to assist clients in their emotional and spiritual development.

Sobel lives near the shores of Lake Michigan with her husband, Tom, and their golden retriever, Kenya. She has two grown children, Amanda and Matthew.

Visit the author's website at www.virginiasobel.com